IMMIGRANTS AND REFUGEES

IMMIGRANTS AND REFUGEES
Trauma, Perennial Mourning, Prejudice, and Border Psychology

Vamık D. Volkan

Routledge
Taylor & Francis Group

LONDON AND NEW YORK

First published 2017 by
Karnac Books Ltd.

Published 2018 by Routledge
2 Park Square, Milton Park, Abingdon, Oxon OX14 4RN
711 Third Avenue, New York, NY 10017, USA

Routledge is an imprint of the Taylor & Francis Group, an informa business

British Library Cataloguing in Publication Data

A C.I.P. for this book is available from the British Library

ISBN-13: 9781782204725 (pbk)

Typeset by V Publishing Solutions Pvt Ltd., Chennai, India

CONTENTS

ABOUT THE AUTHOR

Vamık D. Volkan, M.D., DFLAPA, FACPsa, was born in Cyprus. Before coming to the United States in 1957 he received his medical education at the School of Medicine, University of Ankara, Turkey. He is an Emeritus Professor of Psychiatry at the University of Virginia, Charlottesville, Virginia, and an Emeritus Training and Supervising Analyst at the Washington Psychoanalytic Institute, Washington, DC. For eighteen of his thirty-nine years at the University of Virginia, Dr. Volkan was the Medical Director of the university's Blue Ridge Hospital. A year after his 2002 retirement Dr. Volkan became the Senior Erik Erikson Scholar at the Erikson Institute of the Austen Riggs Center in Stockbridge, Massachusetts, and for the last decade has spent three to six months there each year.

In the early 1980s Dr. Volkan was a member and later the chairman of the American Psychiatric Association's Committee on Psychiatry and Foreign Affairs. This committee brought together influential Israelis, Egyptians, and Palestinians for unofficial negotiations. In 1987 Dr. Volkan established the Center for the Study of Mind and Human Interaction (CSMHI) at the School of Medicine, University of Virginia. CSMHI applied a growing theoretical and field-proven base of knowledge to issues such as ethnic tension, racism, large-group identity, terrorism, societal trauma, immigration, mourning, transgenerational transmissions, leader–follower relationships, and other aspects of national and international conflict. The CSMHI"s faculty included experts in psychoanalysis, psychiatry, psychology, diplomacy, history, political science, and environmental policy. In 1987 the Soviet Duma signed a contract with the CSMHI to examine existing difficulties between the Soviet Union and United States. Later CSMHI members worked in the Baltic Republics, Kuwait, Albania, the former Yugoslavia, Georgia, South Ossetia, Turkey, Greece, and elsewhere. Dr. Volkan founded the CSMHI's journal, *Mind and Human Interaction*, which examined the relationship between psychoanalysis and history, political science, and other fields.

Dr. Volkan was a member of the International Negotiation Network (INN) under the directorship of former US president Jimmy Carter (1989–2000) and also a member of the Working Group on Terror and Terrorism, International Psychoanalytic Association. He was a Temporary Consultant to the World Health Organization (WHO) in Albania and Macedonia. He had the honor of giving the keynote address in Cape Town, South Africa in 2006, celebrating Archbishop Desmond Tutu's life of peaceful justice and the tenth anniversary of the Truth and Reconciliation Commission. He also was honored on several occasions by being nominated for the Nobel Peace Prize, with letters of support from twenty-seven countries. Dr. Volkan holds Honorary Doctorate degrees from Kuopio University (now called the University of Eastern Finland), Finland; from Ankara University, Turkey; and the Eastern European Psychoanalytic Institute, Russia. He was a former President of the Turkish-American Neuropsychiatric Society, the International Society of Political Psychology, the Virginia Psychoanalytic Society, and the American College of Psychoanalysts. He was an Inaugural Yitzak Rabin Fellow, Rabin Center for Israeli Studies, Tel Aviv, Israel; a Visiting Professor of Law, Harvard University, Boston, Massachusetts; a Visiting Professor of Political Science at the University of Vienna, Vienna, Austria; and at Bahçeşehir University, Istanbul, Turkey. He worked as a Visiting Professor of Psychiatry at three universities in Turkey. In 2006 he was Fulbright/Sigmund Freud-Privatstiftung Visiting Scholar of Psychoanalysis in Vienna, Austria. In 2015 he became a Visiting Professor at El Bosque University, Bogota, Colombia.

Among many awards, he has received the Nevitt Sanford Award, the Elise M. Hayman Award, the L. Bryce Boyer Award, the Margaret

Mahler Literature Prize, the Hans H. Strupp Award, and the American College of Psychoanalysts' Distinguished Officer Award for 2014. He also received the Sigmund Freud Award, given by the city of Vienna, Austria, in collaboration with the World Council of Psychotherapy, and the Mary S. Sigourney Award for 2015. The Sigourney Award was given to him for his role as a "seminal contributor to the application of psychoanalytic thinking to conflicts between countries and cultures," and because "his clinical thinking about the use of object relations theory in primitive mental states has advanced our understanding of severe personality disorders."

Dr. Volkan is the author, co-author, editor, or co-editor of over fifty psychoanalytic and psychopolitical books, some of which have been translated into Turkish, German, Russian, Spanish, Japanese, Greek, and Finnish. He has written hundreds of published papers and book chapters. He has served on the editorial boards of sixteen national or international professional journals, including the *Journal of the American Psychoanalytic Association*, and is the Guest Editor of the Diamond Jubilee Special Issue of the *American Journal of Psychoanalysis*, 2015.

Currently Dr. Volkan is the president emeritus of the International Dialogue Initiative (IDI), which he established in 2007. The IDI members are unofficial representatives from Iran, Israel, Germany, Russia, Turkey, the United Kingdom, the United States, and the West Bank. They meet twice a year to examine world affairs, primarily from a psychopolitical point of view. Dr. Volkan continues to lecture nationally and internationally.

A refugee crisis

On the evening of 13 November, 2015 coordinated terrorist attacks in Paris, France killed 130 and injured 368 innocent persons. Seven attackers were also killed. The Islamic State of Iraq and Syria (ISIS), or al-Dawla al-Islamiya fi al-Iraq wa al-Sham [Islamic State of Iraq and the Levant] (DAESH), or simply Islamic State (IS), claimed responsibility for this tragedy, which took place when many European countries were in the middle of a "refugee crisis." During the previous months hundreds of thousands of persons from Syria, Iraq, Afghanistan, and elsewhere were fleeing to Europe, searching for a safe environment. Their numbers were surpassing those of newcomers to Europe during the preceding months and years. Some European leaders thought that Europe, with over 700 million residents, could accommodate new asylum seekers and refugees, and that newcomers might even be helpful in increasing the host countries' economic growth. Others were afraid of being unable to control the situation.

Meanwhile, we repeatedly heard stories of major tragedies. The International Organization for Migration (IOM) reported that up to 3,072 people died or disappeared in 2014 in the Mediterranean while trying to migrate to Europe, and shipwrecks involving refugees continued, such as that of 27 August, 2015, when two vessels sunk off the Libyan coast with 550 migrants on board. More than 400 persons were estimated to have drowned. Some credit this event as coining the phrase "European refugee crisis," used by the media and the public ever since. For some time, the incredible traumas Syrian refugees faced were symbolized by pictures of a drowned three-year-old Syrian boy of Kurdish ethnic background, named Alan Kurdi, which made headlines worldwide. According to news reports, his family boarded a fifteen-foot rubber raft from the Turkish resort town of Bodrum destined for the Greek Island of Kos. The boat capsized killing twelve Syrians. On 2 September, 2015, Alan's lifeless body was found washed up on a Turkish Aegean beach.

Soon after this event the European Union's sharpening divisions over the refugee crisis and some Europeans' fear of newcomers' religious and cultural values "contaminating" local sentiments became more apparent. For example, the Hungarian Prime Minister Viktor Orban warned Europeans that allowing mostly Muslim families to settle in Europe would be a threat to Europe's Christian roots, and Slovakia's government authorities indicated that Slovakia may accept only Christian asylum seekers. Meanwhile, Germany anticipated receiving 800,000 newcomers within a year and declared that it would not ban Syrians from coming. After a while, however, in mid-December, 2015, Chancellor Angela Merkel pledged to substantially reduce these numbers.

Adding to the complexity of the situation, a Syrian passport that belonged to an asylum seeker was found near the body of one of the gunmen after the 13 November, 2015 terrorist attacks in Paris, connecting the Islamic State's activities with the immigrants. The idea that ISIS may be printing Syrian passports and that terror-linked people may pose as refugees spread fear—not only within the host countries in Europe, but also in the United States. More than half of US governors announced they would not accept Syrian refugees in their state. Some politicians and public figures stirred up controversy and created more anxiety by implying that all Muslims in the United States were potentially dangerous.

As terrorist attacks were taking place in Paris, a meeting in Berlin at which I was the speaker, was just ending. This meeting was related to another event that had taken place, also on 13 September, but seventy-two years earlier. We were honoring the memory of John Rittmeister who was born in 1898 in Hamburg. He went on to become a neurologist, a psychoanalyst, and a teacher of many younger colleagues. He resisted the Nazi tyranny, and was associated with the resistance group Red Orchestra (*Die Rote Kapelle*). In late 1942 he was arrested by the Gestapo and accused of high treason. On 13 May, 1943, he was beheaded by guillotine at the Plötzensee prison in Berlin. Adolf Hitler had commanded in 1936 that a guillotine be used at this prison, and one was brought there in 1937. Today we are horrified when we see television images of beheadings performed by Islamic Republic murderers, whose victims must kneel in front of them wearing orange clothes. Rittmeister's story reminds us that people being decapitated has long been a part of human history.

At the meeting, I gave the 2015 Rittmeister Lecture, and I learned about the tragedy in Paris while watching the news on television after returning to my hotel room late that evening. The next day I participated in another meeting entitled "Migration—Social Trauma—Identity," sponsored by the International Psychoanalytic University of Berlin and held in a building only five to ten minutes away from where Syrian and other refugees were located. (Before the winter arrived, around 1,000 people, mostly from Syria, would begin to move and settle in Berlin's old Nazi Airport, Tempelhof, built in the 1930s.) During the meeting there were many references to these refugees. I noted that the audience that day—about 200 persons—made no reference to events in Paris. I sensed that this was not because they lacked empathy. It was because the audience was busy with a wish, almost a need, to express as clearly as possible how different they were from Neo-Nazis and other Germans who were against Germany's acceptance of hundreds of thousands of refugees. The polarization in Germany was disturbing to them. They referred to the Holocaust and how transgenerationally induced shared guilt feelings played a role in their benevolence toward suffering immigrants.

One well-known German psychoanalyst, who had come to the Berlin meeting from another city, told the audience a story. The day before, he had seen some Syrian refugees while riding in a train and was filled with sympathy for their condition. Suddenly a Syrian child, a prepubescent boy, appeared in the train compartment where the psychoanalyst was resting. The boy was searching for an electric outlet to plug in and charge his iPhone. In the psychoanalyst's mind, the refugees needed to be "suffering" people, not rich ones. Noticing the iPhone in the hands of the refugee boy interfered, at least temporarily, with the psychoanalyst's mood and inclination to feel for the refugees, to look after and be good to them. The boy's carrying a valuable item spoiled the psychoanalyst's wish to do something good for suffering individuals. When he noticed his temporary frustration he was embarrassed. His sharing this story with the audience illustrated for me more clearly how the Germans in the meeting room, especially the younger ones, wanted nothing to prevent them from taking care of the suffering of Others and reverse their Holocaust-related guilt feelings.

I found myself comparing what I was observing at this Berlin meeting the day after the Paris attacks with the German society my co-workers from the Center For the Study of Mind and Human Interaction (CSMHI) at the University of Virginia and I had studied before and after the fall of the Berlin Wall on 9 November, 1989 and again in the early 1990s (Ast, 1991; Thomson, Harris, Volkan & Edwards 1995; Volkan, 1990b, 2006, 2013). By the end of 1992, after the tragic events among Serbians, Croats, and Bosnians, Germany accepted 235,000 refugees from the former Yugoslavia. There was an eruption of intense hatred and aggression toward these asylum seekers at that time, and this shared hostile prejudice became combined with xenophobia against the guest workers. In the 1950s and 1960s, West Germany had signed agreements with Greece, Turkey, Morocco, Portugal, Tunisia, and Yugoslavia to recruit workers for West Germany's industrial sector, and by 1973 there were more than one million *Gastarbeiter* in West Germany. These migrant workers also brought their families to join them, including children. What was happening in Germany and other parts of Europe was called "neoracism." This term referred to hatred toward perceived cultural, rather than genetically determined characteristics. Neoracist video games, such as those titled *Concentration Camp Manager* or *Total Auschwitz* were distributed in Germany, Austria, and even Sweden. While Europe was on the verge of an unprecedented era of social, economic, and political cooperation, the evidence of resurgent xenophobia was beginning; bombings, beatings, murders, and discrimination in employment and housing were taking place. The Council of Europe's April 1992 *Report on Racial Violence and Harassment in Europe* focused on neoracism in France, Germany, Italy, the Netherlands, Sweden, and the United Kingdom. It noted that, at the time of the report, only the United Kingdom had officially acknowledged and taken steps to correct the problem. There was no doubt that complex political and economic issues had triggered the spread of neoracism. My colleagues' and my focus at that time was on the underlying psychology of hostile and malignant prejudice.

The German Psychoanalytical Association was prompted to prepare a serious statement on the violence in Germany, which was approved by the General Meeting of the Association held in Wiesbaden on 19 November, 1992. This statement asserted that one underlying reason for the violence in Germany was "the Federal Republic's long outmoded conception of itself as a homogenous nation." From a psychological standpoint, the influx of refugees and other foreigners served to "attack" the self-contained idealized concept that was shared consciously or unconsciously by many Germans. As the Association recognized in its statement, the response was "to make the 'foreigner' the scapegoat—that is, to see him as the source of all grievances and discontent."

This statement called for courage and action by politicians. It reminded everyone that:

> We must all become aware of our xenophobia and learn to integrate psychically that which is alien, where it is in fact in unconscious terms something of our own. Hence tolerance and humanity towards foreigners call for a constant effort of civilization and culture. This is the only way to diminish the power of projections and to mitigate the conception of "us" as a national entity which aggressively excludes others.

The United States is a "synthetic country," to use historian/psychoanalyst Peter Loewenberg's (1991) term, a place where people, even refugees (except African slaves), have come voluntarily from different places with different experiences to create a synthesis of disparate influences and live together. The German Psychoanalytic Association's statement brought to our attention that, in 1992, Germany too was no longer fully homogenous, since people of different origins were already settled there.

In the 1990s, fear of losing local cultural homogeneity in France had a different focus. Sophie Meunier (2000) and Rita Rogers (2000) described how, to the French, globalization in the 1990s was perceived as Anglo-Saxon acculturation and a threat to France's national and cultural values. Meunier reported a story illustrating protest against American-style globalization in France in 2000. In August that year a sheep farmer, Jose Bové, became famous by deliberately destroying a French McDonald's restaurant. Then, as a big celebrity, he made a trip to the Seattle meeting of the World Trade Organization (WTO) and, to show the French superiority over American fast food, smuggled in 400 pounds of Roquefort cheese. Rogers stated: "Because of a fear of losing identity, people become easy prey of vitriolic political arsonists who create for them the identity of belonging to the 'Community of Victims'" (Rogers, 2000, p. 286).

In the 1990s and 2000s, nation states' responses to globalization were not only observable in France and Germany, as similar responses and fear of losing local culture were noticeably taking place in other locations. Homogeneity of many nation states has been impacted in striking ways by globalization, incredible advances in communication technology, fast travel, and now by huge numbers of voluntary or forced immigrations. Today, the largest Muslim community in Europe lives in France, and its existence, especially after the November 2015 Paris attacks, has created immense fear among many French people. During the last World Refugee Day, held in June 2015, annual figures from the United Nations High Commissioner for Refugees (UNHCR) informed us that there are almost 60 million refugees and internally displaced persons around the globe. One in every 122 people worldwide is a refugee or internally displaced person, and half of these are women and children. By July 2015 the number of refugees fleeing war and persecution in Syria rose to over four million. With a population of 77 million, Turkey is today home to about two million Syrians, nearly four times the number there at the end of 2013. A porous Greek frontier has become an entry point for hundreds of thousands of migrants wishing to reach Germany or other parts of the European Union.

The idea of having an ethnically pure national identity or being a synthetic country composed of only *selected* people from *selected* locations is an illusion in our present-day world. It is now vital to investigate and understand benign, hostile, or even malignant prejudice toward the Other—those who have a different ethnic, national, religious, or ideological large-group identity. In this book I will use the term "large group" to refer to hundreds of thousands or millions of individuals who share the same tribal, ethnic, religious, national, or ideological sentiments, even though they will not meet each other in their lifetimes. Large-group identities are the end-result of myths and realities of common beginnings, historical continuities, geographical realities, and other shared linguistic, societal, religious, cultural, and ideological factors. Large-group identities are articulated in terms of commonality, such as: We are Apaches. We are French. We are Catholics. We are capitalists. Or: You are Basque. You are Syrian. You are Sunni Muslim. You are communist.

Infants and very small children are, using Erik Erikson's (1956) term, *generalists* as far as tribal affiliation, nationality, ethnicity, or religion are concerned; the subjective experience and deep intellectual knowledge of belonging to a large-group identity develops later in childhood. Such sharing of sentiments applies as well to those who are members of a politically ideological group to whose ideology their parents and the important people in their childhood environment subscribed. Religious cults like Branch Davidians near Waco, Texas; guerrilla forces such as the Revolutionary Armed Forces of Colombia (FARC); and terrorist organizations such as the Taliban or Islamic State also show us that people can be attracted, in their *adulthood*, to becoming members of a *different type* of large group and assuming new large-group identities. This type of large group exists as long as they have and hold on to a religious, ideological, or terroristic mission they wish to carry out.

In today's globalized world, people from different places can quickly connect with one another. However, this development also influences and often threatens people's investment in their large-group identity. That large groups ask the metaphorical question, "Who are we now?" has become a key issue in present-day world affairs, causing the re-emergence of centuries-old religious and cultural practices in an effort to stabilize a "new" identity and fear of the Other, including a sense of entitlement to kill the Other.

Two days after the Paris attacks, I left my Berlin hotel in the morning to go to Tegel Airport to fly home to the United States. My driver turned out to be an intelligent man in his early forties who had migrated to Germany from Turkey when he was fourteen years old. He belonged to the largest ethnic minority in Germany, one of about three million people having at least one parent who emigrated from Turkey to Germany. Since I was born to Turkish parents on the island of Cyprus before migrating to the United States in my early twenties, I was able to speak with the driver in Turkish and spontaneously "interview" him. His father was a guest worker, and the family had come from a city in Anatolia. My driver had managed to receive a university degree in Germany, but, in the long run, had ended up working as a taxi driver.

He described having many German friends. Yet, he told me that when they went to a bar together, when under the influence of alcohol, they would often use derogatory terms when referring to my driver's ethnic background and then later apologize to him for their nasty behavior. My driver informed me that he could not yet feel fully comfortable living in Germany. He explained that his brief annual visits to his family's city in Turkey have been a necessary activity for him; he seemed to have an obligation to maintain a *link* to his Turkish origin. His sister, whom he loved, was fourteen years younger than him and had been born in Germany. She spoke German without an accent and had become a judge. He compared his adjustment as an immigrant to his sister's adjustment as someone who was German born. Sometimes, at their family home, he would ask his sister to bring him this or that. According to his family's old Anatolian tradition, a younger sibling, especially a sister, would be willing to please a brother fourteen years her senior. My driver expected a positive response from his sister, but instead she would often say, "Why don't you get up and fetch what you want?" He never became angry with her, but always noted how she had given up a Turkish tradition and was behaving like a German. Yet, he added that his sister too was holding on to her family's ethnic identity, saying that she would not marry a German, but would wait to marry a Turk.

On our way to the airport we drove by many restaurants with Turkish names. Sometimes such names were rather long, such as "Best Tasting Turkish Food Place," or the name would identify where the restaurant owner had come from and indicate that the customer would find meals within that were traditional to this location in Anatolia. Still other restaurants referred to an item, such as Masam ("My Table") or Güllü Lahmacun (Pide with Rose) in Turkish. There would be no German translations of these restaurants' names. My driver believed that exhibiting such names was deliberate since, as symbols of their separate identity, they provided links between 200,000 people who had come to Berlin from Turkey.

During the meeting at the International Psychoanalytic University of Berlin, when I noted that the people in the audience were very concerned with the polarization in Germany, I repeatedly reminded the audience that, after a flood of immigrants and refugees, a host country's population usually becomes polarized. Polarization was not only happening in Germany; severe political polarizations related to immigrants and refugees already existed in France, Belgium, the United

States, and elsewhere in the world, such as in Australia. We discussed how psychoanalytic observations of the psychology of refugees, the host countries, and information about shared prejudice, large-group identity issues, and related topics might be helpful in efforts to prevent, or at least tame, future traumas that could affect newcomers as well as local people who will live alongside them. To do so would require that interested psychoanalysts sometimes leave the chairs behind their couches and participate in societal activities. This would also enlarge the horizon of psychoanalysis. We were aware that so far there had been no serious or systematic teaching of large-group psychology in its own right at psychoanalytic institutes and schools. I answered the question, "What does *large-group psychology in its own right* mean?", by explaining that there are echoes of individual psychology in large-group psychology shared by hundreds of thousands, or millions of persons, but we recognize that a large group is not the same as a single, stand-alone person. Nevertheless, multitudes of people in a large group do share psychological journeys, such as complicated mourning after major shared losses at the hand of the Other who belongs to another large-group identity, or when they use the same psychological mechanism, such as "externalization" of unwanted images, that makes the Other a shared target. These journeys become sustained social, cultural, political, or ideological processes that are *specific* for the large group under study. I added that considering large-group psychology in its own right includes making formulations as to a large group's' conscious and unconscious shared psychological experiences and motivations that initiate these specific processes. This is the same method psychoanalysts follow in their clinical practice when they make formulations about the internal worlds of their patients in order to summarize what their diagnoses and treatment will be (Volkan, 2013, 2014c).

My involvement in this meeting and my "interview" with the driver the next day were two events that initiated the idea of writing this book. After all, my studies on refugee issues from a psychoanalytic angle go back some decades, and using information from my earlier experiences may shed light on the present refugee crisis and the ever increasing fear of people from another large group. After the Turkish army divided Cyprus into Northern Turkish and Southern Greek sections in 1974, I studied Cypriot Turks who escaped from the southern part to the northern part of the island (Volkan, 1979). In the spring of 1990 I also spent time with Palestinian refugees. After the 1982 war in Lebanon, the Palestine Liberation Organization (PLO) moved its headquarters to Tunisia. Chairman Yasser Arafat, important individuals of the PLO administration, and many other Palestinians, including 52 Palestinian orphaned children, lived in Tunisia. During my time with them, I especially examined the children's psychology (Volkan, 1990a, 2014b). My next study of refugees and asylum seekers (Volkan, 1990b, 2006, 2013), to which I have already made reference above, took place in Germany. But my most intense work with refugees took place in the Republic of Georgia. After the collapse of the Soviet Union, wars broke out in the early 1990s between Georgians and South Ossetians and also between Georgians and Abkhazians, within the legal boundary of the Republic of Georgia. From May 1998 until March 2002 I went to the Caucuses two or three times a year and worked with internally displaced Georgians and South Ossetians (Volkan, 2006). In the summer of 1999, some 450,000 Kosovar Albanians sought shelter in Albania. In 2000, when I visited Albania as a temporary consultant for the World Health Organization, I met some of them and heard stories of others (Volkan, 2013).

In 2015 I participated in a gathering in Malaysia titled, "The Malay Leadership Mystique: Building a Background to a Psychoanalytic Understanding of Malay Leadership Qualities in Politics and Business." I was very impressed that some very influential people in Malaysia were gathered at this event and that they had also asked four psychoanalysts from Europe and the United States to join them, to examine what they call "the Malay Dilemma," which describes the influence of old migrations far back in the country's history. They wanted to explore the role of psychologically informed education and other peaceful methods for changing society. The Malay people lived under Others for four centuries and won their independence in 1957. Subjugation to feudalism and colonialism for centuries affected Malay cultural traits, traits that are still present in modern Malaysia. After the British began ruling the Malay states in 1786, Chinese and Indians searching for livelihood migrated to Malaysia. In his book titled *The Malay Dilemma* the former prime minister of Malaysia Mahathir Mohamad (2012) notes that, "In Malaysia, we have three major races which have practically nothing in common. Their physiognomy, language, culture and religion differ ... They live apart in different worlds—the Chinese in the towns, the Malays in the *kampongs* and the Indians on the estates. Nothing makes anyone forget the fact of race. So those who say 'forget race' are either naïve or knaves" (pp. 220–221). I observed how migrations that occurred centuries ago can still affect a country's social, political, and cultural issues. Article 160 of the Malaysian Constitution, in a sense, answers the question "Who are we now?" A Malay is defined as "a person who professes the Muslim religion, habitually speaks Malay, conforms to Malay custom, and: (a) was born before Merdeka Day [31 August, 1957 independence day], in the Federation or Singapore or born of parents one of whom was born in the Federation or Singapore, or was on Merdeka Day domiciled in the Federation or Singapore: or (b) is the issue of such a person."

On 2 December, 2015 two Muslims—Syed Rizwan Farook, a US citizen, and his Pakistani wife, Tashfeen Malik, a permanent resident—opened fire in San Bernardino, California during a party in the Inland Regional Center, killing fourteen people and wounding twenty-one. The couple were later killed in a shootout with police. "Since 9/11, over 400,000 people have been killed by gunfire in America and 45 by jihadist violence, of whom half died in two shootings: one carried out by a Muslim army doctor in Texas in 2009, the other in San Bernardino" (*The Economist*, 2015, p. 29). The San Bernardino killers' ISIS sentiments and the arsenal found at their home helped to further generalize fear of danger from unexpected persons at unexpected locations, home-grown "wolves," with Muslim jihadist sentiments. During this time, daily discussions in the American news media about banning non-US citizen Muslims from entering in the United States played a role in inflaming fear among the US population, but also increased references to American "values" and its constitution.

Four days after the San Bernardino tragedy, regional elections took place in France. Boosted by fear about security and immigration, the extreme-right National Front (FN) won more votes than any other party. On 13 December, 2015 during the regional election runoff, however, the National Front failed to win any region. On New Year's Eve, as crowds gathered around Cologne Cathedral to welcome 2016, groups of North African and Middle Eastern men accosted women. According to news reports, two women were raped. We also learned that on the same night similar events had taken place in other cities, from Hamburg to Helsinki.

On 22 March, 2016 three coordinated attacks occurred in Brussels, Belgium, killing 32 bystanders and three attackers, and injuring over 300 individuals. ISIS claimed responsibility for these attacks. Fear of mass Islamification and what became known as "Eurabia" spread, leading to expectation of more Paris- and Brussels-style and Cologne-style events in Europe.

Political, social, economic, legal, cultural, religious, and medical aspects of the present-day refugee crisis in Europe and elsewhere in the world involve a complexity of border crossing problems, settlement programs, health issues, and security matters. It is beyond my expertise to examine the realistic, practical aspects of having a huge number of "outsiders" settling in host countries. As a psychoanalyst, however, I also try to learn about such realistic considerations.

* * *

This book is divided into two parts. In Part I, my main focus will be on the psychology of the newcomers, both voluntary and forced immigrants. I will review psychoanalytic theories concerning immigrants and refugees. I will present detailed clinical findings on mourning and its complications as a preparation to examining immigrants' and refugees' responses to loss of persons and things of their original locations. I will describe perennial mourning and the evolution of linking objects and linking phenomena as expressions of this condition. I will give examples of newcomers' linking objects and phenomena and their various utilizations, and case examples of the impact of traumatic experiences, age-factors, large-group identity issues, and transgenerational transmissions on newcomers' adaptation to their new lives. I will also illustrate how a dislocation experience becomes intertwined with a person's existing psychological developmental issues and unconscious fantasies.

In Part II my attention will turn to people in the host countries or locations to which internally displaced individuals escape. I will examine the host population's reactions toward newcomers, especially toward a flood of refugees. An observation of an analysand's prejudicial outbursts over a one-and-a-half-week period in the fourth year of his analysis is presented in order to illustrate how several psychological factors can combine to make an individual preoccupied with prejudice against persons who have their own historical and cultural customs and belong to another religion. I provide a detailed description of the evolution of prejudice, especially collective prejudice, against the Other with a different large-group identity, in order to explain the psychology of such collective responses. I will give illustrations of how physical borders can become psychological borders protecting large-group identities.

The importance of psychoanalysts' experiences in examining societal and political matters and their search for ways to communicate their findings to other mental health workers, educators, professionals dealing with refugee crises, and the public in general, will be addressed throughout the book.

PART I

NEWCOMERS

CHAPTER ONE

Psychoanalytic theories on adult immigrants and refugees

There are many variables involved in the immigration experience. Newcomers differ in respect to their ages, psychological makeup, and the support system that is available to them. Babies and small children, without having stabilized object constancy of people, pets, and things left behind, cannot be "typical" immigrants or refugees like their parents. León and Rebecca Grinberg (1989) stated that, "Parents may be voluntary or involuntary emigrants, but children are always 'exiled': they are not the ones who decide to leave and they cannot decide to return at will" (p. 125). In this chapter I write about adults as dislocated persons.

Dislocation takes place on a spectrum, ranging from "forced immigration" (a term that does not do justice to the actual tragedy of Africans brought to America as slaves and their descendents, or at the present time people escaping places such as Syria), to the voluntary immigration of individuals seeking a better life for themselves and their families. In cases of voluntary immigration, integration into a new country is generally smoother than the adaptation by a refugee, if the individual's psychological makeup does not present complications. A refugee is in the position of feeling pressured, consciously and unconsciously, from the outset of relocation to prove that, "he is worthy of the mercy

3

bestowed on him by the land that receives him. He lives with an urgent need to assimilate and to adapt. His rage against the land which he was forced to leave makes him repudiate and repress many attachments of the past. He feels guilt toward those whom he left behind in danger" (Wangh, 1992, p. 17). These factors combine to frustrate a person's integration into a new country and culture. Obviously, the situation is more tragic and even more complex in cases of "forced immigration."

There is one key common element that underlies the psychology of all dislocated individuals. Since moving from one location to a foreign location involves losses—loss of family members and friends; loss of ancestors' burial grounds; loss of familiar language, songs, smells, food in one's environment; loss of country; loss of previous identity and its support system—all dislocation experiences can be examined in terms of the immigrant's or the refugee's ability to mourn and/or resist the mourning process.

Sigmund Freud's (1917e) "Mourning and melancholia" deals with internalized object relations. It refers to an *adult mourner*'s internal work dealing with the images of a lost object and the fate of the mental representation of this object. Here I use the term "representation" to refer to a collection of images. Mourning refers to an individual's intense internal review of images of lost persons or things until this preoccupation with associated affects loses its intensity. The extent to which an individual is able intrapsychically to accept this loss will determine the degree to which an adjustment is made to a new life. In this chapter I will review some key papers and books written about psychodynamic issues of immigrants and refugees, and in the next chapter I will look at the psychology of mourning in detail and closely examine the complications that may be associated with the mourning process.

For a long time, the psychology of immigrants and refugees was not studied extensively by psychoanalysts. This is surprising, since there were and are many psychoanalysts who were or are immigrants themselves. In my book *A Nazi Legacy*, I reviewed multiple reasons why, until recent decades, psychoanalysts in general have been hesitant to examine in depth the impact of external events on their analysands' internal worlds (Volkan, 2015). I believe that one major reason for this is that many Jewish psychoanalysts escaped from the Holocaust as refugees themselves, and many of them became key figures and important teachers in psychoanalytic training facilities. As Rafael Moses and Yechezkel Cohen (1993) stated, "the wish not to have terrible events be true, not to have them touch us, not to be too closely aware of what took place" (p. 130) was the most significant reason these psychoanalysts avoided, or even denied, the role of tragic historical events in their lives. Peter Loewenberg (1991) and Leo Rangell (2003) also reminded us that some aspects of a large-group history induce anxiety. Psychoanalsys who are Holocaust survivors or their offspring had to deal with anxiety. Vera Muller-Paisner (2005) remembers stories about her miraculous birth as a first child to a Holocaust survivor who was forty-four years old. But there were holes in her family's story. Only later did she learn how her Jewish parents had reinvented their lives after the Holocaust. She wrote: "Family tapestries that hide the fabric of lies about collective traumas keep a person from knowing where they come from and who they are" (2005, p. 15). In the United States, three well-known psychoanalysts whom I know, Henri Parens (2004), Anna Ornstein (Ornstein & Goldman, 2004) and Paul Ornstein (Ornstein & Epstein, 2015) talked or wrote about their experiences as survivors of the Holocaust and refugees only after many decades had passed.

In 1974 Cesar Garza-Guerrero from Mexico, who was trained in the United States, wrote about immigrants who do not experience major trauma during dislocation. He stated that the immigrants experience "culture shock" (Ticho, 1971) due to the sudden change from an "average expectable environment" to a new and unpredictable one. By referring to "average expectable environment," Garza-Guerrero was describing Heinz Hartman's (1939) perception of an environment that is responsive to a child's psychological needs. According to Garza-Guerrero, the adult immigrant activates a fantasy that the past contained all "good" self- and object images, along with their gratifying affective links. When the reality of dislocation sets in, such mental images are felt to be missing. At some point, the immigrant feels disconnected from "good" object images and experiences a sense of discontinuity. Not only do family members, friends, and other individuals exist in one's "average expectable environment," but non-human objects do as well.

The significance of non-human objects in one's environment was emphasized by Harold Searles (1960). Later in this book I will describe the moving story of a Georgian refugee family. The family members, stepping over dead bodies, had escaped from Abkhazia during the Georgian-Abkhazian war of 1992–1993 and had become internally displaced people who settled at Tbilisi Sea, near the capital city Tbilisi. The daughter of this family, then in her mid-teens, would not and could not swim in the lake at the family's new location, because, she insisted, this lake was not the Black Sea where she had enjoyed swimming during her earlier life in Gagra, a city in Abkhazia. Longing and nostalgia for the Black Sea, a non-human environment, would not allow her to enjoy swimming in the lake at her new home.

The initiation of a mourning process changes culture shock. According to Garza-Guerrero, once the immigrant whose mourning process can proceed without complications works through the mourning for what has been abandoned, this person can form a new identity that is neither total surrender to the new culture nor the sum of bicultural endowment. The new identity will be reflected in a remodeled self-representation that incorporates selective characteristics into the new culture that have been harmoniously integrated or that prove congruent with the cultural heritage of the past.

If the immigrant still feels accepted in the country left behind, upon completing the mourning process, for practical purposes she may experience biculturalism, resulting in a sense of belonging to neither culture to the exclusion of the other. In fact, this person will belong "totally to both" (Julius, 1992, p. 56). Greek-American Demetrios Julius states: "I slowly came to an appreciation of the importance of intrapsychic cultural complementary and, more significantly, to an acceptance of the vast cultural differences of the two countries [Greece and the United States]. I began to accept certain psychological paradoxes and to feel myself truly bicultural" (ibid.). Sentiments expressed by Garza-Guerrero and Julius find support from scholars in other fields. For example, historian Dina Copelman (1993) stated that the majority of Americans were at some point the immigrant, the refugee, or the Other, and wrote: "Instead of assuming that cultural and psychological health rest on possessing coherent, unified identities, I want to explore what it might mean to accept—even to celebrate—the fact that the immigrant is likely to remain a citizen of two (or more) worlds" (p. 76).

When I came to the United States from Cyprus in my early twenties after medical school in Turkey, I had already secured a job as a medical intern in a hospital. I had planned to return to Cyprus after completing my training in psychiatry, but then chose instead to stay in the United States. In the long run, I would become like Demetrios Julius and Dina Copelman, and feel comfortable experiencing myself as "truly bicultural." But, during my initial years in this new country, my psychological journey to achieve this state of mind was complicated due to a deadly ethnic conflict between Cypriot Greeks and Cypriot Turks in the country I had left behind. My roommate when I was in the last years of my medical school in Ankara, a young man with a promising future who was also from Cyprus, was shot and killed by a Greek terrorist a few months after I arrived in the United States. He was attacked at a pharmacy where he had gone to buy some medicine for his ailing mother. This event induced guilt feelings in me: I was alive and my roommate was dead. Also, I was living in safety in the United States and my family members on the island were living in an enclave under subhuman and unsafe conditions, surrounded by their enemies. My mourning process of voluntarily leaving one location and moving to another one had become complicated (Volkan, 1979, 2013).

There was also another factor that would prohibit me from feeling as comfortable as Demetrios Julius or Dina Copelman as a "truly bicultural" person. They had come to the United States as children and learned to speak American English without an accent, whereas I had, and continue to have, an accent when speaking English. León and Rebecca Grinberg, having been "transplanted" on several occasions and worked in three countries, are also qualified as "participant-observers" in real immigrant and refugee matters. They have studied language development theory and the impact the mother–child relationship has on it, especially in cases of separation. They describe the newcomer's psychological resistance to changing from the native language, and conclude that age is a factor. Children seem able to identify with a new cultural environment relatively quickly, and are capable of letting the new language sink in. For adult immigrants, the age factor makes the task far more difficult, and they may never succeed in acquiring the "music" (accent, rhythm) of the new tongue. The Grinbergs state that the task of learning a new language is a major problem for any immigrant, especially an adult; this is a highly vulnerable area where defensive mechanisms play a major role (Grinberg & Grinberg, 1989).

Since I have an accent when speaking English, I will always be recognized as a "foreigner" in the United States. Living in the US for decades has also influenced my accent while speaking Turkish. When visiting Turkey or North Cyprus during the last couple of decades, there have been dozens of times when a person in a marketplace or a hotel has expressed admiration for my Turkish and asked where I learned to speak it so well. I usually tell them that I had no choice in learning Turkish since my mother taught me this language when I was a child.

It is questionable whether or not we should consider an adult's voluntary emigration to be a traumatic event. "Trauma" comes from the Greek word for an invasive wound. Laplanche and Pontalis (1967) summarize Freud's conceptualization of trauma. According to them, trauma for Freud "connotes a violent shock, a breaching or breaking through a protective shield and the consequences of such a shock and its invasive effects upon the psychic organization as a whole" (p. 465). I do not object to thinking of voluntary emigration as a traumatic event because of its links to culture shock, losses, and struggle for adaptation. However, situations of forced exile and other traumas, including life-threatening ones, will complicate mourning and adaptation. I refer again to León and Rebecca Grinberg, who wrote what was, to my knowledge, the first comprehensive psychoanalytic study of both migration and exile in book form, published in 1984 in Spanish (English version: Grinberg & Grinberg, 1989). Their psychoanalytic understanding of persons who are voluntarily or involuntarily dislocated was based on Melanie Klein's (1940, 1946) theories. Klein had the idea that an infant at birth has capacity for some ego functions and experience of anxiety. She believed that at the beginning of postnatal life the infant can feel persecutory anxiety due to external and internal sources. She perceived the experience of birth as an external attack on the newborn infant and referred to Freud's (1920g) "death instinct" as the internal source of persecutory anxiety (Klein, 1950). She believed that the infant projects love and hate to the mother's breast, creating a "good" and a "bad" breast, a "good" or "bad" object. The bad object as a terrifying persecutor can induce persecutory anxiety. The infant develops what Klein called "depressive position" after he integrates the mother's (her breasts') "good" and "bad" representations. Klein assumed that this position starts developing in rudimentary form at four to six months and continues throughout the life of the individual. Losing an "all good" internalized image gives rise to sorrow and certain painful fantasies, in that aggression may destroy needed and loved objects. The possibility of losing the good object leads to guilt. If an individual cannot deal with depressive anxieties he may develop "manic defenses" in which fantasies of controlling objects emerge, or may experience a regression to the earlier "paranoid-schizoid position" associated with splitting, projective identification, omnipotent denial, and idealization.

Klein's theoretical explanations were perceived as controversial by some psychoanalysts. For example, Sandor Lorand (1957) noted: "Surely one of the prime requisites of an adequate theory is economy of explanatory concepts—a good theory should give the simplest explanation which does justice to the facts. This requirement appears to be violated by Kleinian theorists" (p. 285). Nevertheless, the "Kleinian school" of psychoanalysis developed with many followers. It is true that psychoanalytic theories on aggression go all the way back to Freud's various thoughts on this topic before 1920, followed by his ideas about the "death instinct" (Freud, 1920g), a notion today's psychoanalytic literature has little use for.

At the present time most considerations on aggression fit into Henri Parens' (1979) "multi-trends theory of aggression." Parens states that the way parents rear their child is a direct factor in that child's aggression profile, while he also considers the role of a child's average-expectable biological conditions in this profile. The quality of attachment and the child's aggression profile are linked. Parens describes a wide range of expressions of aggression, from anger to hostility, to rage, to hate.

Returning to the Grinbergs' theories explaining immigrants' and refugees' adjustments, we see how anxieties may appear in persecutory or depressive forms. They showed how feelings of guilt over loss of parts of self (i.e., the immigrant's or the refugee's previous identity, his or her investment in the people, and the land left behind) may complicate the immigrant's mourning process.

When the newcomer's guilt is "persecutory"—that is, the individual is driven by guilt to expect punishment from others—the principal emotions are pain, despair, fear, and self-reproach. He or she often confuses past and present and also becomes prone to pathological mourning. If the individual acknowledges the loss of the past life intrapsychically and is able to accept the pain (Kleinians call this "depressive guilt"), the individual may exhibit sadness, sorrow, or nostalgia but will still be able to retain reparative tendencies and responsibility, and discriminate between past and present. The immigrant or refugee who has depressive guilt rather than persecutory guilt is usually better equipped to adjust to a new life. In the case of forced immigration, the individual's own psychological organization usually generates more persecutory guilt than may be found in the individual who becomes an immigrant by choice. After all, the refugee's guilt is reinforced by being a survivor, while relatives and friends may have been killed or remain in danger. If either the immigrant or the refugee faces discrimination within the host society, however, persecutory anxieties are kept alive or may be rekindled (Wangh, 1992).

The Grinbergs refer to emigration as a traumatic experience that "comes under the heading of what have been called cumulative traumas and tension traumas, in which the subject's reactions are not always expressed or visible, but the effects of such trauma run deep and last long" (Grinberg & Grinberg, 1989, p. 12). They note that those left behind, like those departing, utilize various unconscious defense mechanisms to deal with the pain of their loss. While the Grinbergs acknowledge the mourning process experienced by the newcomer, their emphasis is on exploring the various types of guilt and anxiety encountered during the dislocation experience. Although the psychodynamics of mourning was not stressed in their pioneering work on migration and exile, in another volume León Grinberg (1992) continues to refer to mourning.

Another psychoanalyst, Salman Akhtar, who migrated to the United States from India in his adulthood, saw immigrants' adaptation according to Margaret Mahler's (1968) concept of "separation-individuation" (see also Mahler, Pine, & Bergman, 1975) and Peter Blos' (1968, 1979) ideas on adolescent "second individuation." Akhtar (1999a, 1999b) argued that the immigrant's adaptation constitutes a "third individuation;" the first having occurred in childhood and the second during adolescence. Before turning to this theory of third individuation, let me first summarize Mahler's and Blos' findings.

Mahler presents four subphases of separation-individuation. She calls the first subphase "differentiation." It refers to the child's moving out of the symbiotic unity with the mother (or mothering person) from four–five to eight–nine months. From ten to fifteen months of age the child is in a second subphase, called "practicing." With emerging cognitive and motor skills the child experiences physical and psychological separation from the mother while needing her availability for "emotional refueling." Mahler's third subphase is known as "rapprochement." From about sixteen to twenty-four months the child begins to realize some harsh realities of life. For example, the child realizes that he cannot control the mother; he is not omnipotent. The child becomes involved in a situation of wishing for the return of the symbiotic bliss with the mother that existed prior to the start of separation-individuation and his attempts to individuate further. The child experiences dependence as well as flights away from dependence. Fantasies and conflict related to anal and pre-oedipal issues are involved in the relationship between the child and the mother during this subphase. Then, starting at twenty-four months and ending at thirty-six months, the child is in the last subphase of separation-individuation. This subphase is known as "on the road of object constancy." When the child is capable of developing a stable libidinal mental representation of the mother, he can experience the same security and comfort as when the mother is physically present.

Anna Freud (1958), Edith Jacobson (1964), and others have discussed the regression of the ego and superego in adolescence, which precedes the new integration that crystallizes the formation of character. This regression occurs in the service of development. It is involuntary and, as Peter Blos (1968, 1979) puts it, is developmental phase-specific regression. He describes how "second-individuation" occurs as the adolescent loosens the tie to infantile object images and corresponding self-images. According to Blos (1968), "Adolescent regression in the service of development brings the more advanced ego of the adolescence into contact with infantile drive positions, with old conflictual constellations and their solutions, with early object relations, and narcissistic formations. We might say that the personality functioning which was adequate for the protoadolescent child undergoes a selective overhaul" (p. 180). Blos also describes how during the adolescent passage, identifications with new friends or groups take over superego functions, episodically or lastingly. He suggests that residual trauma—residuals of conditions that were unfavorable to development when the person was younger—are assimilated in the character formation during adolescence. Lastly, he states that during the adolescence passage a person works on correcting distortions in the family history and develops a stable sexual identity.

In 2009 Akhtar introduced the term "third individuation", which is related to the identity transformation consequent upon immigration. He wrote:

> ... the "third individuation" has only a phenomenological resemblance and not a genetic equation with the infantile processes it is named after. Much psychic structuralization has ensued by the time the "third individuation" takes place. Drives have attained fusion and gained genital primacy. The ego is better organized and postadolescent superego is in place. The term "third individuation",

therefore, links an adult life reorganization of identity to a childhood phenomenon in a playful and metaphorical way. However, the potential of reworking earlier separation-individuation conflicts through this process cannot be ruled out. (pp. 286–287)

My own studies on the conditions of dislocated persons have primarily focused on the newcomers' ways of mourning, their capability and/or difficulty delegating the mental representations of what has been lost (family, land, identity) to the realm of "futureless" past memory (Tähkä, 1984), or their becoming "perennial mourners" and utilizing linking objects and linking phenomena in maladaptive or adaptive and even creative ways.

CHAPTER TWO

Mourning and perennial mourning

Mourning is an obligatory response to a significant loss. Adult immigrants and refugees are obliged to carry out a review of images of what they left behind. In some cases such a process seemingly stops preoccupying the individual's mind in the long run; in other cases such preoccupations, in one way or another, remain active. Because response to the loss of a significant object, once initiated, moves through different recognizable phases, we can easily assume that if the passage through any of these is complicated, an immigrant or refugee may be fixated at that particular stage. In that event, manifestations expectable in that stage will be exaggerated, and the individual's psychological state will be further complicated by reflecting the complications as well as adaptations.

In this chapter I will focus on individuals whom we see in psychotherapy or psychoanalysis whose clinical pictures reflect various manifestations after the loss of an important person. Death is the most concrete of losses. In our response to it we see the residue of all other incomplete, forced, or hurried separations. By reviewing observations of how people respond to the death of a significant person, we can prepare ourselves to examine immigrants' or refugees' reactions to losses, not only losses of individuals they leave behind or individuals who die while escaping with them, but also losses of land, familiar things, security, honor, and prestige. Their reactions to such losses, especially in cases of forced immigration, are usually linked to other traumas. After examining aspects of mourning in this chapter, in the chapters that follow I will tell stories of newcomers' responses to dislocation experiences including, in Chapter Seven, the story of a refugee family five years after they had to escape to a new location.

Psychoanalysts who contributed to the literature on mourning have mainly focused on reactions to the loss of a person, and they have divided the mourning process into different stages. George Pollock (1961, 1989), for example, classified the mourner's reactions into two states: acute and chronic. He held that the first goes through three sequential steps of its own: a) shock, accompanied by denial of loss; b) acute grief (affective) reaction; and c) separation reaction, which reflects withdrawal of psychic interest in the internal representation of the lost person or thing. This is followed by a chronic state with various manifestations of adaptive mechanisms. The mourner attempts to integrate the experience of the loss with the reality so that life activities can go on. Pollock seems to equate his chronic stage with Freud's (1917e) work on mourning. Bowlby and Parkes (1970) came up with four stages of mourning, again, mostly by describing responses to the loss of people. The first stage involves numbness, which is interrupted by outbursts of intense distress and/or anger. According to Bowlby and Parkes this stage lasts from a few hours to a week. Their second stage includes yearning and searching for the lost figure. They indicate that this stage may last for months or years, during which the mourner will not only yearn for the one lost but be aware of an urge to search for that person. Then comes a phase of disorganization, followed by a fourth and final stage, which is one of at least some degree of reorganization.

I have also divided adult reactions to a significant loss into two phases: a) the grief reaction, and b) the work of mourning. My clinical studies of various types of grief reactions and mourning processes of individuals began in the late 1960s (Volkan, 1972, 1981; Volkan, Ast and Greer, 2002; Volkan, Cilluffo and Sarway, 1975; Volkan and Josephthal, 1980; Volkan and Zintl, 1993). After I was involved in international relations I spent more time studying societal mourning. This manner of dividing human reactions to the significant loss of a person was also mentioned by psychoanalytically informed historian Norman Itzkowitz. He wrote: "Although dictionaries give grieving and mourning as synonymous, for me they are not the same emotionally. To grieve and experience sorrow that accompanies it is a much more transitory matter than mourning. Mourning is a process, and you have to go through the entire process and emerge at the other end before you can let go of the deceased. As such, it takes time. Dictionaries neither grieve nor mourn, otherwise they would know the difference" (Itzkowitz, 2001, pp. 173–174).

Erich Lindemann (1944) long ago pointed to what he called "anticipatory grief," the gradual accommodation one makes to the loss of a significant other whose life is clearly coming to a close, and to the passage through some or all of the stages of grief that may in such circumstances take place before the actual event of death occurs. The grief reaction includes a sense of *shock* if the mourner was not prepared to lose a psychologically significant person (or thing). The sense of shock alternates or is accompanied by numbness and/or some physical reactions such as shortness of breath, tightness in the throat, a need to sigh, muscular limpness, and a loss of appetite. As shock and its physical symptoms abate, the mourner experiences a wish to have the loss reversed. She may deny, at least for a while, that the loss actually took place. A more common phenomenon is the mourner's utilization of splitting. The term "splitting" used here is not the same as that of borderline individuals. Borderline individuals typically split their self-images and/or object images. The mourner splits an ego function, so that opposing perceptions and experiences can take place simultaneously (Freud, 1940e). For example, a woman knows that her dead husband is lying in a coffin at a funeral home. But this same grieving widow "hears" her husband's car as it crunches the gravel in the driveway. Grief reaction also includes the mourner's bargaining with "God," "Fate," oneself, or others in order to reverse the death of someone or to undo the burning of a beloved house, as if such reversals were possible: "If I were not stuck in traffic and home earlier, I would have prevented the accident that caused the death of my wife." The mourner, in his mind, may become preoccupied with the idea of taking a different route when driving home that day and avoiding the heavy traffic. Or the mourner may dream of reversing the tragedy in other ways.

But in reality the lost person (or thing) never reappears and the mourner feels guilty, to one degree or other, for not reversing the outcome of the tragedy and/or for continuing to live while someone else is gone or something is destroyed. The mourner's own guilt, however, is complicated because—again, to one degree or another—there is also anger that, by being lost, someone or something induced in the mourner a narcissistic wound. The lost person (or thing) will no longer respond or satisfy the mourner's wishes. Often the mourner displaces anger onto someone or something else, such as a widower might direct his resentment toward a physician who had taken care of his dead wife. Most importantly and obviously, a mourner's grieving is accompanied by pain and sorrow. A mourner, in a sense, keeps hitting her head against a wall, a wall that never opens up to allow the dead person (or lost thing) to come back. This itself induces anger, but this type of anger is a healthy indication that the mourner is beginning to accept the facts. My research has shown that there is no connection between the degree of initial anger and the chronicity of complications during grief reaction. The person who seems to be having a dramatically angry response may just as dramatically recover from this anger and follow a more usual course of mourning.

A typical grief reaction takes some months to disappear. In truth, there is no typical grief reaction, because the circumstances of a loss are varied, and because each individual has her own degree of internal preparedness to face significant losses. Grief reactions may also reappear for a time at the anniversary of the event when the loss took place.

A grief reaction can itself be complicated. There are adults who spontaneously cry and feel pain and anger whenever something in their environment reminds them of their original loss. Once I had an analysand who spent the first two and a half years on my couch crying and exhibiting a grief reaction at each session. After grieving for a while she would become interested in other topics that had nothing to do with her loss. But during her next session she would grieve again. She was fixated in grief.

Before grief is completed, the work of mourning begins. This phase of mourning involves a slow process of revisiting, reviewing, and transforming the mourner's emotional investment in the images of the lost object. While the individual continues to relate and review images of the lost person, as Freud (1917e) stated, the mourning process results in the mourner's identifications with some of these images and their realistic and/or fantasized functions. Such identifications can be enriching. A widow who had depended on her now dead husband to look after the family's financial matters becomes an expert in handling money a year after her husband's death. The indolent son of a lawyer has an urge to enroll in law school after his father's death.

When the relationship between the mourner and the object mourned had been ambivalent and stormy, the mourner's reactions are apt to be complicated by a variety of component feelings and thoughts. The disruptive identifications may take place. Disruptive identifications that are invested with deep ambivalence cause "melancholia," a profoundly painful dejection and a cessation of interest in the external world (Freud, 1917e). The struggle between wishing to keep the ambivalently related internalized image or representation of the lost object and wishing to get rid of it may lead to suicide, an act that in this case unconsciously represents the mourner making a stronger attempt to get rid of the image or the representation of the lost object, which is now internalized within the mourner's self-representation.

Classical psychoanalysis considered a "normal" mourning process to last a year or so following the loss. A mourner, however, does not identify, in healthy or unhealthy ways, with all mental images of the lost person. Many unassimilated mental images of the lost person remain available to the mourner. It is theoretically better to link the completion of a "normal" mourning process to the mourner's making the mental representation of the lost person or thing "futureless" (Tähkä, 1984, 1993). When the object representation of the lost item has no future, the mourning process comes to a practical end. A young man stops fantasizing that a wife who has been dead for some time will give him sexual pleasure, for example. Mental images of the lost object may be temporarily activated only during some special occasion, such as when a young woman dreams the night before her wedding day about her dead mother. Since unassimilated mental images of lost objects remain in our psyche even when they are tamed, shrunk, repressed, or denied, adult-type mourning, in a sense, does not end until the mourner dies (Volkan & Zintl, 1993; see also, Kernberg, 2010).

My studies on mourning have illustrated that complications in one's mourning process do not always lead to "melancholia" (depression), but may result in another outcome called "established pathological mourning." Adults suffering from this become *perennial mourners,* doomed to remain preoccupied with aspects of their mourning process for decades to come—even until the end of their own lives. Perennial mourners experience their mourning without bringing it to a practical conclusion. There are various degrees of severity of such a condition.

Some perennial mourners live miserable lives; others express their unending mourning in more creative ways, but even some of these people, when not obsessed with their creativity, feel uncomfortable.

Now I will illustrate the internal map of a person who becomes a perennial mourner. To a large degree, such a mourner cannot identify sufficiently with the selected enriching aspects of the object representation of the lost item. On the other hand, the mourner does not end up identifying totally, with both love and hate, with many object images of what is lost. In other words, the mourner cannot go through a "normal" mourning process or develop "melancholia." Instead, the perennial mourner keeps the object image or representation of the lost person (or thing) within her self-representation as an attention-seeking and *unassimilated* "foreign body." In the past we called such a specific and influential unassimilated object image or representation an *introject*. An identification with the introject does not take place, and the object image or representation, with its own "boundaries," remains in the individual's self-representation. The ambivalent relationship of the past continues in the mourner's involvement and preoccupation with the introject; the mourner is torn between a strong yearning for the restored presence of the lost person (or thing) and an equal wish that the lost item become futureless. The presence of the introject provides an illusion of choice, and in this way it reduces anxiety. But, having an introject also means the continuation of an internal struggle with it. Such an introject excessively influences the person who has it.

I noticed that the term "introject," used by psychoanalysts such as Gustav Bychowski (1952) decades ago, does not appear in contemporary literature. I think that we should revive it. It fully describes the situation as it appeared in the following perennial mourner.

A man came to see me complaining that his younger brother had been disturbing him daily and he did not know how to deal with the situation. He sought treatment in order to free himself from his brother's influence. He explained that while driving to work in his car his brother constantly talked with him, even when my patient wanted some time for himself or when he wanted to listen to the car radio. His brother gave him advice about everything. For example, he made suggestions as to how my patient should behave when meeting his boss or when talking to a particular secretary at work. My patient did not like his brother's advice. Sometimes he told his brother to shut up, but the younger man continued to talk and irritate him. I also learned that when both men were young my patient experienced considerable sibling rivalry.

I pictured my patient in his car with his brother sitting next to him. I even imagined that my patient and his brother lived together in the same house or at least nearby, which would explain their riding together each workday to the downtown business area. I was, therefore, very surprised when my patient, in his sixth therapeutic session, informed me that his younger brother had died six years earlier in an accident. The "brother," with whom he had conversations while driving to work, was actually his brother's unassimilated specific and attention-seeking object image or representation. My patient felt it to be lodged in his chest. Sometimes he experienced this object image or representation as a puppet-sized younger brother sitting on one of his shoulders, literally a symbolized burden on his shoulder. But most of the time, the "brother" was inside my patient's body image. My patient carried on his internal conversations with his brother's introject.

If a mourner has an "introject" of the lost person (or thing) and interacts with it, this does not make the mourner a psychotic individual. For example, outside his special "relationship" with his younger brother's introject, my patient simply had a neurotic personality organization. He did not experience any break with reality except when communicating with his introject. An established pathological mourning may *imitate* a psychotic condition, and a clinician needs to be alert to this, taking care not to confuse it with schizophrenia or related excessively regressed conditions.

A perennial mourner daily expends energy to "bring back to life" or "kill" (make futureless) the lost person (or thing). Again, the severity of this preoccupation varies from individual to individual. In severe cases this struggle renders the mourner's adaptation to daily life very difficult. Perennial mourners are compulsive about reading obituary notices. This betrays not only anxiety for their own death, but an attempt to deny the death of the one they mourn because they find no current mention of it. Some such mourners fancy they recognize their lost ones in someone alive whom they encounter at a distance. They make daily references to death, tombs, or graveyards in a ritualistic way, and talk about the dead in the present tense. Listeners get the impression that the speakers' daily life includes some actual relationship with the deceased who continues to watch over them.

Perennial mourners have "typical dreams." They can be classified as follows:

- "Frozen" dreams: Many perennial mourners spontaneously use the term *frozen* to describe the fixation of their mourning processes and also to describe some of their dreams, which are often composed of what appears to be one slide after another, with no motion taking place upon any of them. The term "frozen" also reflects lifelessness.
- Dreams of life-and-death struggle: In these, the dreamer sees the one who has died or is lost as still living or existing, but engaged in a life-and-death struggle. The dreamer then tries to rescue the person— or to finish him off. The outcome remains uncertain because the dreamer invariably awakens before the situation in the dream can be resolved.
- Dreams of loss as an illusion: For example, the perennial mourner dreams of seeing the dead body but noticing something about it, such as sweat, that denies the reality of death.

Returning to my patient, it will be recalled that sometimes he felt that a little "figure" was sitting on his shoulder. This imagined figure was an *externalized* version of his brother's introject. In 1972, after studying fifty-five individuals suffering from complicated grief reactions and/or mourning processes, I coined the terms "linking object" and "linking phenomenon." Briefly, these terms describe some mourners' externalized versions of introjects of lost persons (or things). My patient "created" this imaginary figure and it was his *linking phenomenon*. Through experiencing a figure on his shoulder, my patient connected himself with his dead brother. Sometimes, for a perennial mourner, a song, a hand gesture, even a certain type of weather condition functions as a linking phenomenon. It was raining on the day a young woman attended her father's funeral. The song "Raindrops keep falling on my head" came to her mind. Later, she utilized this song as a linking phenomenon whenever she felt internal pressure to mourn.

Most individuals with established pathological mourning, however, utilize certain concrete inanimate objects (such as a special photograph) or even sometimes animate objects (such as a pet), that symbolize a meeting ground between the object representation of a lost person or thing and the mourner's corresponding self-image. I call such objects *linking objects*. Mourners "choose" a linking object from various items available in their environment. A linking object may be a personal possession of the deceased, often something the deceased wore or used routinely, like a watch or camera. A gift the deceased made to the mourner before death or a letter written by a soldier on a battlefield before being killed may evolve into a linking object. A realistic representation of the lost person, such as a painting, can also function as a linking object. Then there is what I call a "last-minute object," a thing at hand when a mourner first learned of the death or saw the dead body. They relate to the last moment in which the deceased was regarded as a living person. For example, a woman had a horrible car accident. She survived and was able to get out of the badly damaged car, but she witnessed that her young daughter who had been sitting next to her was dead. The woman picked up a stone next to the damaged car and put it in her purse. This stone became her last-minute linking object. Sometimes linking objects are "selected" later, after an individual becomes a perennial mourner, but once an item truly evolves as a linking object, the perennial mourner experiences it as "magical." The mourner may hide it, but needs to know the linking object's whereabouts; it must be protected and controlled. If a linking object is lost, the perennial mourner will experience anxiety, often severe.

Through the creation of a linking object or phenomenon, the perennial mourner makes an "adjustment" to the complication within the mourning process; the mourner makes the mourning process "unending" so as not to face the conflict pertaining to the relationship with the object representation of the deceased. By controlling the linking object, perennial mourners control their wish to "bring back" (love) or "kill" (hate) the lost person, thus avoiding the psychological consequences if any of these two wishes are gratified. If the dead person comes back to life, the mourner will depend on this person forever. The gratification of this wish would have a negative consequence. If the dead person is given up, the mourner's existing anger will cause feelings of guilt, and thus the gratification of this wish too would have an unwelcome ending.

More importantly, since the linking object or phenomenon is "out there," the mourner's mourning process too is externalized. Mourners do not feel the struggle with the introject within themselves. The linking object in the external world contains the tension between ambivalence and anger pertaining to the narcissistic hurt inflicted by the death. When mourners "lock up" in a drawer a photograph that has become a linking object, they also "hide" their complicated mourning process in that same drawer. All they need is to know where the photograph is and that it is safely tucked away. They may unlock the drawer during an anniversary of the loss and look at the photograph or touch it. But as soon as they feel anxious, the photograph is locked up again.

Linking objects and phenomena should not be confused with childhood transitional objects and phenomena that are reactivated in adulthood. Certainly there are some regressed adults who utilize the transitional relatedness of their babyhoods over a lifetime and/or recreate transitional objects or phenomena (Fintzy, 1971; Volkan, 2010). A transitional object represents the first not-me, but it is never totally not-me. It links not-me with mother-me and it is a temporary construction toward a sense of reality and security (Greenacre, 1970; Winnicott, 1953). Linking objects and phenomena must be thought of as tightly packed symbols whose significance is bound up in the conscious and unconscious nuances of the complicated internal relationship that preceded a significant loss. These objects and phenomena are associated with mourning in childhood only after the child has established object constancy and has a mental representation of the Other, even though this representation may still not be firmly established or may be primarily fantasized.

Linking objects and linking phenomena should not be confused with keepsakes. Not every child's teddy bear is a transitional object, and neither is a mourner's every keepsake a linking object. Adults without complicated mourning cherish keepsakes to remember a lost person or thing. A keepsake does not function as a repository where a complicated mourning process is externalized, but typically provides continuity between the time before the loss and the time after the loss, or *generational continuity* if the lost person or item belonged to a previous generation. On the other hand, a linking object is a psychological "tool" utilized for dealing with complicated mourning. A dead person's framed picture on a mantle with which the mourner is not preoccupied is a keepsake. When a mourner, even many years after the loss, is preoccupied with a similar picture by ritualistically touching it at certain times while developing tears, or locking it in a drawer while experiencing anxiety whenever the drawer is unlocked, or being unable to travel long distances without first placing the picture in a special location in the baggage to take along, we can assume that this picture now is a "magical" tool utilized to maintain complicated mourning. If, in the future, the perennial mourner is able to make the lost person's representation "futureless," then the picture loses its "magic," and becomes a "typical" keepsake.

Initially in my decades-long clinical study on mourning, I focused on the pathological aspects of linking objects and phenomena. Since I was working with psychiatric patients with perennial mourning, I considered the existence of linking objects or phenomena only as a sign of mourners' externalizing and "freezing" their mourning process. Even then my colleagues and I thought about utilizing linking objects and phenomena in the therapeutic setting to bring the externalized and locked-up mourning back into the patients' internal worlds to be unlocked and restarted (Volkan, 1981; Volkan, Cilluffo & Sarvay, 1975; Volkan & Josephthal, 1980). Later I began noting that some perennial mourners gained useful time through their utilization of linking objects and phenomena. I learned that keeping a sense of belonging to the past as well as a foot in the future (where the lost person [or thing] will no longer be present) can be a helpful transition for these individuals when circumstances change. In contrast to perennial mourners who remain in a pathological state the rest of their lives, those who are able to use this gained time to reinternalize the meaning of the linking object or phenomenon often may reactivate a "normal" mourning process years after the loss through use of their linking objects or phenomena. They may eventually function as more healthy mourners (Volkan, 2014b). At this time they usually throw away their linking objects or turn them into keepsakes.

CHAPTER THREE

Newcomers' linking objects, linking phenomena, and nostalgia

Immigrants, internally displaced persons, and refugees exhibit various aspects of grief reactions and manifestations of the mourning process described in the previous chapter. If persons significant to them do not die while they are escaping from one location to another one, the newcomers focus more on the loss of the "average expectable environment," which includes not only people but also non-human objects and sometimes pets. We need to consider the historical and political environment in studying the newcomer's mourning process. In the United States I have met many individuals, mostly elderly persons, who, after settling in the United States, never went back to their original countries to see their parents and relatives. Even when they were voluntary immigrants, historical and economic factors prevented them from making visits to their homelands. Today, with the means to travel quickly, visiting places left behind is much easier, unless there are politically induced obstacles. Recently I worked with an Iranian man who had been jailed by the Iranian authorities six years ago due to his political ideas. After he managed to escape from Iran to a country in Europe with his wife and child, even though he wanted to go back to his original country, if only for short visits, he could not do so or he would risk being caught and jailed again. Although he has a

25

comfortable professional position in the new country, he is spending time and energy to find legal and political means to visit Iran. His situation obviously affects his mourning process. The Universal Declaration of Human Rights of 1948, Article 13(2), states: "Everyone has a right to leave any country, including his own, and to return to his country." A person's inalienable human rights, if they may be exercised, help to facilitate the internal ability to mourn. In today's world such rights are taken away from many who are escaping to other countries voluntarily or involuntarily.

There are refugees, even voluntary immigrants, who exhibit aspects of grief reaction, sometimes years after dislocation. I studied the psychological adjustment to a new location of three Uyghurs, one couple and one single man, who had escaped from the Xinjiang autonomous region in China to North Cyprus. With great emotion, including anxiety, they described the inhumane treatment they had received at the hands of the Chinese authorities. By this time they had been living in North Cyprus for a little over a decade and they expressed their relief that they had come to this place. All had repeating "frozen dreams." In many dreams they were in their original homes and preoccupied with people and items in their original environment. Each had obvious guilt feelings for leaving loved ones behind. Every time they remembered and verbally described an item important to them from the country they had left behind, or a special event that had taken place prior to their dislocation, tears came to their eyes.

The most common psychological condition of dislocated persons is their exhibiting various aspects of being perennial mourners. Sometime after I came to the United States in 1957 I bought a photo album and placed in it the pictures I had brought with me of myself, my family, my friends, and my environments in Cyprus and Turkey. On the first page of this album I wrote, "My Life Before Coming to America." Each time I moved to a new place in the United States—a year in Chicago; five years in Chapel Hill, North Carolina; and then Charlottesville, Virginia—I put this album in a drawer (and once in an attic) away from me, hiding it. When I came to Charlottesville in 1963, I was on the faculty of the University of Virginia's Department of Psychiatry. After I started my work with patients with complicated mourning I realized that I was using my "magical" album as my linking object. Apparently, without realizing its personal meaning for me, I had found a way to externalize my mourning process for settling in a new country. Earlier in this book I described how my roommate was shot by a terrorist in Cyprus soon after my arrival in Chicago. At that time I did not have close friends in my new location with whom I could express my feelings and thoughts about this event and work through them. My initial adaptation to life in America was complicated. In a book that I wrote with Elizabeth Zintl, *Life After Loss* (Volkan & Zintl, 1993), I described how, in the long run, I was able to mourn as a "normal" newcomer. Here is that story:

> In 1973, I, with historian Norman Itzkowitz from Princeton University, started working on the psychobiography of Kemal Atatürk, the founder of the Turkish Republic. It took us five years to write *The Immortal Atatürk: A Psychobiography* (Volkan & Itzkowitz, 1984). It is no accident that the writing took us so long. As a Cypriot Turkish child I perceived Atatürk as my charismatic father figure. The odyssey toward understanding him led me to mourn my series of losses due to my emigration to the United States and leaving behind the Cypriot Turkish culture, which was dominated during my young years by Atatürk's modernization efforts. I also mourned the recent death of my father, who had been a great admirer of Atatürk. In *Life After Loss* I described a dream I had on the night of a celebration to mark the publication of *The Immortal Atatürk*:
>
> The night of publication party, I dreamed that I was surrounded by newspapers in many languages. However, the headlines were understandable to me because they were all the same: "Atatürk is dead," and I was sobbing. Atatürk represented my father, my Turkish identity, my traditions and roots. With the completion of this book and that dream, I laid to rest old issues that lingered even after my analysis. I felt more comfortable and integrated as a Turkish-American. (Volkan & Zintl, 1993, pp. 142–143)

When I started to work with immigrants, refugees, and internally displaced persons (IDPs) who had been living in a new location for some time and were no longer under the direct impact of grief reactions and struggles related to new settlement, I easily noticed that they often had linking objects or phenomena. In the introduction to this book I wrote about how the driver who took me to the airport in Berlin had a *need* to make yearly visits to Anatolia, as it was his way of maintaining a *link* to his childhood life in Turkey. He also described to me how the

Turkish names of many restaurants, without German translations, were important for the Turks living in Berlin.

As expected, the development of perennial mourning varies from one newcomer to another for many reasons. In some cases the impact of perennial mourning is very mild; in other cases characteristics of this condition are very prominent. When an immigrant, refugee, or internally displaced person uses a linking object or phenomenon in a creative way, she connects with the lost persons, things, locations, or culture; makes efforts to give them up; renders them "futureless;" and moves on. The adaptive use of a linking object or phenomenon gives such a person time to work on denial of what is lost, to accept changes, and to realize what may be gained.

Some immigrants or refugees, however, become pathologically preoccupied with their linking objects and phenomena to the degree that they do not have much energy left to spend on finding new ways of living. If their original language evolves as their linking phenomenon they will have a difficult time learning a new language. I noted in more than a few cases how a psychological struggle over losing and wishing to re-find what was left behind was generalized. For example, sometimes people would talk about a persistent habit of losing keys for their apartment or car, when such luxury was available to them, and then finding the lost items in unexpected places. They would have souvenirs, sometimes minor and unexpected ones like an empty bottle, of places they had escaped from, which were placed in special locations in their crowded environment and always protected.

When refugees or internally displaced persons share the same traumas and/or newcomers live together in the same camp or settlement area, they may share the same linking objects or phenomena. A moving example of this, in an art form, has been illustrated by Wolf Werdigier, a well-known painter in Vienna, Austria. Werdigier's father was a Jew who had lost his wife and son during the Holocaust and later married Werdigier's German mother. Owing to his background, I believe, Werdigier has been very interested in human nature, group violence, the Middle East conflict, and psychoanalysis. During the 1990s and in the 2000s, he painted works reflecting dozens of psychoanalytic concepts such as large-group identity, phobia, and linking objects. One of his paintings, titled *The Power of Soil*, shows the agonized face of a man with his eyes closed and his mouth open. Below the man's neck, his body disappears into yellow soil. There are old-fashioned door keys stuck in the ground surrounding the head of this individual. Werdigier explained to me that the inspiration for this painting came from the fact that many Palestinians symbolize their house keys as linking objects (Volkan, 2006). When the Israelis bulldozed their homes these people, in a sense, became internally displaced persons even though they did not leave Palestine. They became perennial mourners over the loss of their homes. They gave the keys psychological meaning in order to "freeze" their mourning process: the hope that they might rebuild their homes and the expectation for revenge are locked up in the keys. Later, pins shaped as keys became a shared symbol for many Palestinians who, I noticed, would wear them on their coat lapels at international meetings.

In the introductory chapter I mentioned my visit to Tunisia in 1990. In 1982, the Palestinian Liberation Organization (PLO) moved to Tunis, Tunisia, after Israelis forced them out of Lebanon. In 1990 the PLO allowed me ten days to study orphaned Palestinian children, refugees in Tunis, who were housed by a humanitarian organization in a home called Beit Atfal al-Sumud (Volkan, 1990a). This home for orphaned Palestinians housed fifty-two boys and girls ranging in age from eight to eighteen years. At this time I was the chairperson of the American Psychiatric Association's (APA) Committee on Psychiatry and Foreign Affairs, and I was encouraged by Israeli colleagues to observe these orphans and then present my findings at a meeting in Jerusalem. I met one handsome seventeen-year-old whom I will call Farouk; he had lived in this orphanage for eleven years. He was the captain of the soccer team and spoke perfect English. When Farouk was five years old he had witnessed the killing of his father, his mother, his sister, and a cousin in Palestine. Farouk and his uncle were the only survivors. Later he was separated from this uncle and with the PLO's help was exiled to Tunisia. He told me his life story in a matter-of-fact way and informed me that he no longer remembered his parents' faces. He confessed that when alone he often wept. "I know it is a healthy thing to do," he said.

While Farouk was talking, he was involved in an unusual activity. He kept rubbing his right shoe. When I became curious about what he was doing, he told me that as a child, while watching his mother and grandmother cook sweets, he had accidently stepped in a hot pan and burned his right foot. His father had put ointment on the burn and tried to soothe his pain. This was Farouk's earliest memory. He still had a scar from this episode and, without my asking him to do so, he removed his right shoe and sock, showed me the scar, and demonstrated his tender way of touching it. The scar covered the lower part of his right foot. He confided that when he touched his scar, "I almost recall my parents from within, from inside my body." He had recently received a scar on his left knee while playing soccer, but he said this was nothing; the old scar was everything.

Listening to Farouk I realized that his scar stood for his lost parents, family, and home. By touching his scar he could bring lost relatives and home back to his life; by not touching his scar he could say "goodbye" to them. Farouk had an ability to sublimate. He was a star soccer player, scoring more goals than anyone else, using his foot with the special scar, and perhaps discharging feelings of rage and revenge in this way. The other orphans seemed to be aware of the specialness of Farouk's scarred foot. They would come and touch his right shoe and sometimes his scar, and their self-esteem and sense of well-being would increase. I realized that Farouk's scar was his linking object, and others at the orphanage were sharing this "magical" part of his skin as their linking object (Volkan, 2014b).

I learned another story of a "living linking object," from Palestinian refugees in Tunis, one that refers to the feeling of nostalgia as a linking phenomenon. At the time of my visit, the PLO had its headquarters in Tunis, and a significant population of Palestinians, including Chairman Yasser Arafat, lived in Tunisia at that time. As a group, the Palestinians seemed to be in a state of perpetual alert and were afraid of unexpected secret attacks by Israeli commandos. Indeed, prior to my visit, one of Mr. Arafat's closest associates had been assassinated at his home during an Israeli raid. I had the impression that most of the Palestinians never had a good night's sleep. They would call or visit each other at all hours of the night just to check that nothing was amiss. Chairman Arafat, I was told, would never stay long at one location, but would move around constantly for security reasons. The PLO used souped-up civilian cars that sped through the streets as if in perpetual motion. The group's anxiety was palpable. The Palestinians in Tunis felt as if they had been forcefully exiled and yearned to return to a peaceful homeland. Even though the Tunisian government had given the PLO certain autonomy, Palestinians in Tunis considered themselves refugees. Over ten days I visited many Palestinian homes and the offices of high-ranking officials. At times I felt that I was being indirectly questioned by the PLO to ensure that I would present my findings in a neutral way.

It was not a secret that I planned to publish my findings and to speak about Palestinian orphan children living in Tunis at an upcoming meeting in Israel on children of war.

During a luncheon with senior PLO officials I met an extraordinary woman in her twenties who asked to be interviewed. For four evenings she came to my hotel and we talked late into the night. Our conversations totaled over sixteen hours, and I took extensive notes. The young woman introduced herself to me in perfect English as the daughter of an airplane hijacker. When she was an oedipal child her father had hijacked a commercial airplane and forced it to land in Israel, demanding the release of certain Palestinian prisoners from Israeli jails. According to her account, her father was "tricked" by Israeli anti-terrorist forces and shot to death during the hijacking episode.

Although the woman gave me permission to use her name, I refrained from doing so when I originally wrote about her (Volkan, 1999), and I will refrain from doing so now. Her story was a poignant one that revolved around being raised with a "hero ghost," the mental representation of her father. After his death, many of his friends who had high positions in the PLO treated her as a special being. She was idealized as a martyr's daughter and a symbol of Palestine. These influential men helped with her schooling; she gradually spent more and more time at PLO headquarters and also functioned as a secretary to Chairman Arafat. She was present at many official and social gatherings of PLO authorities and accompanied them on various travels. When I attended a long luncheon given by Chairman Arafat, for example, she functioned as a kind of silent hostess. My focus here is not to present her personal story per se, but rather to show how she played a significant psychological role for the PLO authorities and, by extension, for the "exiled" Palestinians in Tunis.

Every Palestinian in Tunis knew who she was. When I met her, this woman was young and beautiful, and aware that she represented an idealized Palestine to which the exiled Palestinians wanted to return. When she came to her interviews with me, she wore a white dress. Despite her physical beauty and grace, and despite being regularly pursued by men, she had remained "pure." She wanted me to know that she was still a virgin. I report this to emphasize that she embodied the concept of "virgin white." Even though the Arab–Israeli conflict had been a bloody one and both sides had used violence, this young woman needed to remain like a flower on the battlefield. I learned that many men at PLO headquarters found her very attractive, but she remained, in a sense, "unreachable," representing the Palestinians' longing for their own state, which at that time was also unreachable.

As our hours of interviews were coming to an end, I asked her why she had volunteered to come and tell her story late into the night, to reveal her personal wishes and fears, in short, why she would open so completely to a stranger. She responded that while she was aware of her role as a "flag" for the Palestinian people in Tunis; she also knew that she was made of flesh and blood and had dreams of finding a mate, marrying, having sex, and being a regular person. The fact was that she wanted to be both an idealized symbol, shared by Palestinians "exiled" to Tunisia, and a regular woman. She was aware that in order to be one type of person, she would have to give up the other. Having no solution for her internal struggle, she had developed a daydream in which she would lose both identities to escape the tension. In her daydream, she imagined being in an airplane with Chairman Arafat, her living hero/ father figure. Their plane would explode in midair, killing both of them. Psychoanalysts may infer other meanings to the woman's daydream, such as a wish for reunion with her dead father image, but here I simply want to address her inner struggle between being a symbol or a regular woman. Her fantasy bothered her. She was well read and knew something about psychoanalysis. Thus, when I, a psychoanalyst, appeared in Tunis, she wanted to share with me her internal dilemma, thinking that such sharing might help. Interestingly, she knew that I would not give her any advice.

Many years have passed since I met this woman. To this day, I do not know if my empathic understanding of her internal struggle was helpful to her. Of course, dramatic events relating to the PLO's political situation have taken place since then. The Declaration of Principles (DOP), an agreement between the PLO and the Israeli government, was signed by Yasser Arafat and Yitzhak Rabin in the White House Garden in Washington, DC, on 13 September, 1993. Arafat returned to Gaza on 1 July, 1994. Perhaps the return of Palestinians from Tunis to their ancestral land removed the external pressure on this woman to serve as a physical representation of nostalgia for an idealized Palestine. However, while the DOP recognized the PLO as representing the Palestinians, it did not acknowledge the political and national rights of the Palestinians. Serious doubts emerged about the prospects of establishing a Palestinian state or even allowing the Palestinians the right of self-determination. The fundamentalist movement gained new support among the Palestinians at the expense of the PLO leadership, and identification with the PLO declined. Yasser Arafat, who was also the President of the Palestinian National Authority, died on 11 November, 2004 in Clamart, France.

Historians who focus on the history of the PLO will probably never mention the role that this woman played at PLO headquarters in Tunis in the late 1980s and early 1990s. Maybe they will never wonder how a group of exiled people in the midst of political maneuvering, terrorism, death, and anxiety made this person a "living linking object." As a mental representation of their idealized state and what it meant to them, she helped these Palestinians tolerate the emotions associated with being deprived of it. She served as a link between their idealized Palestine and the reality of its non-existence (a loss).

Some analysts, such as Anzieu (1984), Chasseguet-Smirgel (1984) and Kernberg (1989), describe the mental representation of a state as a nurturing mother figure. The PLO and Palestinians in Tunis had created a literal illustration of this concept. The young woman was both an unreachable virgin, which reflected the reality of their situation, and a future "mother." She was a catalyst for their belief in a hopeful future. I perceived that they used her image to give them strength to move on and seek their statehood.

The Palestinian woman's story illustrates how a living human being may function as a living linking object—in her case, a shared linking object for a whole group of people, the Palestinian community in Tunis. She represented an external meeting ground between the "lost" but idealized Palestine and the reality of being exiles. By keeping their idealized Palestinian state alive in the symbol they created in this young woman, they were inspired not to give up their quest for an independent Palestine. From the point of view of affects, this young woman stood for the Palestinians' nostalgia. Their yearning for her represented nostalgia for a Palestinian state.

Nostalgia is the affect attached to linking objects and phenomena or which may itself function as a linking phenomenon. David Werman (1977) described how a person enjoys the process of searching, while knowing that what was lost will not be found. When used creatively, nostalgia provides a period of time for the immigrant or refugee to make adaptations to a new country. When such adaptations take place, the affect of nostalgia fades away, but usually does not disappear entirely.

By contrast, there are situations where nostalgia cannot even evolve. A refugee or immigrant may openly or indirectly enter a depressed state and be filled instead with affects such as self-pity, resentment, envy, and despair, as is often the case among those who have been traumatized by war and forcefully exiled. The guilt of surviving when others did not, and the sense of helplessness and humiliation, are internalized and overpower hope for the future. When nostalgia is poisoned, it prohibits the gradual process of working through losses and changes, and the individual cannot adapt to a status of refugee or exile, cannot achieve an internal distinction and continuity of past, present, and future. As a consequence, he or she may develop symptoms or character traits to cover up such a lack of internal distinction and continuity.

CHAPTER FOUR

Relocated children and their unconscious fantasies

B efore focusing on immigrants and refugees who are children, first let us look at how children react to loss. Very small children do not have a firmly established mental representation of another person (or thing). As described long ago by Robert Furman (1973) and Erna Furman (1974), young children cannot mourn as adults do. Preoedipal children who lose important figures in their lives sense that something is missing, a sensation not unlike the feeling of being hungry. In order to understand how any given small child is likely to react to a significant loss, such as the death of a parent, there are a number of considerations: the child's age, the type of loss, the security of the home environment, the ability of the adults to provide substitutes, and innate resiliency. The more experience a growing child had with the lost person or thing, and the more she is able to maintain the mental representation of the one who has been lost, the closer the child's mourning will be to an adult's. Even though they learn what death is on one level, very young children's belief in its reversibility remains, however hidden it may be. Pre-adolescent children will have a realistic concept of death and its finality.

As David Dietrich (1989) stated, for a small child a lost parent becomes a "lost immortal" figure—a haunting experience. Over the last twenty-five years I have interviewed and worked with dozens of members of the American World War II Orphans Network (AWON) when they were in their fifties or sixties (Volkan, 2014b). For many members of AWON, their fathers had died in the war before they had been born or while they were infants, and they had no conscious memories of the lost parent. Later, as children, they had been told stories about the fathers they never knew, seen pictures of their fathers, or read about them. Thus, with the help of persons in their immediate environments, these members of AWON slowly created mostly or totally "fantasized mental representations" of their fathers. These representations responded to the children's needs, wishes, fears, and identity formation processes. Since their fathers had died or disappeared amidst wartime circumstances that had increased nationalistic pride, most of the time such fantasized mental representations were grand, very rigid, and mysterious. Correspondingly, as children, most of these AWON members had experienced their own self-representations as "special." They felt different from other children whose fathers were still alive, or even from children whose fathers had died from natural causes or accidents. As adults, most of them still had fantasized grand mental representations of their fathers, which affected them in different ways depending on their other life experiences.

Young immigrant or refugee children without the stabilized object constancy of people, pets, and things lost, also possess fantasized mental images of what was left behind. Because of this they cannot be examined in the same way that we would examine "typical" immigrants or refugees like their parents. Salman Akhtar (1999a) tells us that, "If the parents' decathexis of the country of origin in the months before leaving and their anxiety and mourning upon arrival in the new country is profound, then the young child might lose much needed ego support and suffer adverse consequences" (p. 3). The case of Madhu, outlined by Jennifer Bonovitz and Rebecca Ergas (1999), clearly describes this situation. Madhu was thirteen months old when she and her family emigrated from India to the United States. She came to therapy at the age of fifteen. Her case illustrates how pre-migration disruption of the mother–child relationship, and the mother's post-migration depression, contributed to Madhu's ongoing difficulty in tolerating affects and experiencing high levels of positive emotion. When her parents brought her to treatment they had no idea that the several months preceding emigration and the first two years in the United States were primary factors in her difficulties at the age of fifteen. Madhu's parents believed that their child had been "too young" to be affected by the immigration experience.

The maternal grandmother had become Madhu's primary caregiver during the four months prior to emigration, because both parents had been preoccupied with the move. Madhu's mother described her life during the first two years after the family arrived in the United States as a "black hole" in her memory. She also told her daughter's therapist that her daughter had slept in her crib a lot during this time and that she sometimes forgot little Madhu was there.

Madhu's therapist describes how, during Madhu's treatment, with the help of a photo album, they visited the patient's first year of life. In a sense, the therapist wanted to learn about Madhu's *fantasized* images of what was left behind. The therapist was struck by Madhu's gaze aversion when they came to photos of her with the grandmother, aunts, uncles, and cousins. The patient did not want the therapist to make comments about them. The patient said: "I know they're my family and that we used to live with them, but when I look at them now I feel nothing ... All the warmth has gone out of me" (Bonovitz & Ergas, 1999, p. 19). The authors do not state that Madhu's affective experiences stirred up by immigration at age thirteen months were the sole cause of her difficulties at age fifteen, but certainly little Madhu was deprived of growth-promoting experiences prior to emigrating and for two years after while the family was dealing with immigration issues. The authors also worked with other immigrant families and found that "it is not uncommon for parents to overlook, minimize, or misunderstand their children's affective experience of the move" (p. 19).

We are not informed about what kind of unconscious fantasy concerning her and her parents' immigration experience Madhu developed as she grew older. By mentioning "unconscious fantasy" I am referring to a child's developing an "understanding" of a traumatic event or a series of traumatic events according to the phase-specific ego functions available to the child and according to her relations with important others involved in the traumatic event. The child also contaminates this "understanding" with primary process thinking. This "understanding," initiated by an external event or series of events, is a collection of cognition, affect, danger signals, wish fulfillment, and defenses against wishes that is influenced by whichever psychological developmental tasks the child is dealing with at the time. It does not refer to a formed logical thought process. It is difficult to put a childhood unconscious fantasy linked to a specific event in the child's mind into sentences without intensive psychoanalytic work.

The child's adjustment to life at a new location is influenced by her own unconscious fantasies, as well as conscious ones if she is not too young, and the nature of actual external traumatic events that accompany the child's dislocation experience. In the last chapter I referred to three Uyghur refugees in North Cyprus. Two children belonging to the Uyghur couple, aged eight and nine when I met them, had only fantasized mental representations of the Xinjiang autonomous region in China, which included both very fearful and very loving images. Because of their parents' inability to mourn, the children's internal relationship with their fantasized images of their parent's original environment and land were very active, absorbing a great deal of their psychic energy. However, I could not learn the content of their unconscious fantasies related to their parents' original land because the interviews I conducted with them were brief.

Now I will describe aspects of one of my adult analysands, Manuel, to illustrate that when a child is forced to leave one physical location and go to another, the internal issues dealt with are not left behind. The new physical dislocation impacts the internal processes *above and beyond* issues linked to the mourning process. In Manuel's case, his unconscious fantasies linked to his dislocation experience can be put into words and came to life through many of his actions. His case also illustrates how being born to newcomers to the United States affected him.

Manuel, a handsome man with dark complexion, was thirty-six years old when he came to see me. He was a lawyer. He had been married for eight years to a blond woman of Swedish ancestry, and the couple's only child, a son, was two years old. Manuel told me that his parents had come from Mexico and settled in a rundown Mexican-American neighborhood in a big city in Texas. I learned that his mother had a fair complexion and spoke English well since she had emigrated when she was a child. Manuel's father had arrived in the United States from Mexico as a young man and therefore spoke English with a heavy accent. He also had a darker complexion. When Manuel's parents married, his mother was twenty-eight years old and his father was thirty-six. One year after their marriage, Manuel was born to this Catholic immigrant family. His only sibling, a sister, had been born when he was six years old.

When he visited me, Manuel and his family were living far away from his parents' home in Texas. Manuel was maintaining a ritualistic yet distant relationship with his parents and sister. Mother and son would reassure each other of their special, "mutual love" in telephone conversations that Manuel would cut short whenever his father came to the phone. He wanted to be proud of his parents, but they were still living in the rundown Mexican community as immigrants, and knowing this was stressful for him. He said that his marriage was a good one and that he loved his son. He and his wife had a friend who had been in analysis and this friend had told them how his life had been improved by undergoing psychoanalysis. Manuel was seeking analysis to improve his relationship with his parents and his sibling.

During our initial interview I concluded that in spite of the stress he placed on his embarrassment related to his immigrant parents, he might have unresolved oedipal conflicts and sibling rivalry issues. I also thought that his analysis would be rather routine. However, I was unable to fit a new analysand into my heavy schedule at the time Manuel came to talk with me. I told him it would be at least a year before I could do so, and urged him to seek another psychoanalyst. He replied that it would serve him to wait and that another year would find him in a better financial position to afford treatment. Nevertheless, I was surprised when he called me a year after our first meeting. He became my analysand. I remember thinking that one of the reasons he wanted to wait in order to work with me was the fact that I have an accent when speaking English. Since I thought that he had unresolved oedipal issues, symbolically I would fit well with the image of his oedipal father, who was also an immigrant who spoke English with an accent.

I experienced another and greater surprise when Manuel told me that during the year he had awaited analysis, he had kept by his bedside a picture of me from one of my books, which he had purchased after our first meeting, and that he had "conversations" with it each night. I realized that in my physical absence, during the year before we commenced work together, he had started his "analysis" by himself. We were starting out with a *built-in transference* (Volkan, 2010; Volkan, Ast & Greer, 2002; Werman, 1984).

Consider a patient with a history of one or more treatments in which experiences with, expectations of, and feelings toward the analyst or therapist were not explored in much depth or detail. As this patient enters a new treatment, it is likely that he will carry what I call a built-in transference. That is, the person may unconsciously relate to the present analyst as an extension of—and thus not clearly separate from—the past analyst or therapist, even if the capacity to distinguish between them intellectually is intact. The new analyst, who was not present in the patient's previous treatment, naturally has no (or very little) knowledge about the experiences, expectations, and feelings unexplored there, factors that may carry over into their work together. In turn, the patient, although unaware of it, is anticipating certain responses from the analyst, and yet is puzzled when the analyst does not behave in a particular way.

Here I will not give details of Manuel's life history and his analysis, but will focus on our understanding of the primary reason why his keeping my picture by his bedside for a whole year and "talking" with my image was related to his childhood experience of being exiled for six months. I will also illustrate how his rather typical unconscious fantasies dealing with oedipal issues were used defensively and repeated in many actions to deny and cover up a deeper murderous unconscious fantasy related to a rejecting mother.

Even before Manuel's birth, his father was overseas serving as a soldier in the US Army during the Second World War, although he never saw combat. When Manuel was born he was cared for by his mother and maternal grandmother, the latter dying when he was three years old. Manuel did not have memories of his grandmother, but he was told that she, also an immigrant from Mexico, spoke English with a heavy accent and was a strict person, slapping her daughter even after she was mature, demanding obedience. While pregnant with Manuel, his mother fell; she was consequently bedridden for some months, and cared for by her mother and other female relatives in the Mexican community of the city where they lived. A difficult delivery with forceps caused a painful urinary infection and Manuel's mother would recount the story of her travail over and over again, telling her son, "You're alive because of me." Manuel's mother overfed her infant son. When his father returned to the United States after the war, Manuel, who was almost four years old, felt very anxious about being in a room alone with his father, who in reality, as I learned later, was not punitive. The boy imagined that his father was trying to break up the "intimacy" between mother and son by encouraging him to go out into the streets to play with other boys, although the neighborhood was a rough one.

When Manuel was six years old, his sister was born. The little boy was then sent in a propeller-driven airplane with a female teenage chaperone to rural Mexico to live with his paternal grandmother and other relatives whom he had not met before. He kept the image of the airplane ride in his mind the rest of his life. It was rough and, as the plane shook in the air, he felt that he might die. Suddenly he found himself in a foreign land with relatives who did not speak English. After his arrival in Mexico, he packed his suitcase every day with the idea that he would be taken back to his mother, but it was six months before he was allowed to return to his parental home. While in Mexico, he felt as if he were "exiled." While describing this event to me Manuel continually sobbed.

Within a few months of starting his actual analysis with me, Manuel described his awareness of how he had repeated his childhood "exile" experience by keeping my photograph at his bedside and talking with my image every night while waiting to see me again. And his coming to me after one year was like an angry child's homecoming; he was a different Manuel. No longer was he a gentle, polite lawyer. As an adult he had spent some years as a soldier in a war zone, and he would come to his sessions as if he were dressed in a military uniform. On the surface he was seeing me as a dangerous oedipal father. In his sessions he would use the same words to describe me and his childhood father—a scary figure who might punish him. I learned that while he was having his "analysis" with my picture, he had embraced celibacy. This would help him to hide his incestuous oedipal fantasies.

From childhood, Manuel had unrepressed sexual fantasies about his mother. He believed that at times she watched him through the keyhole of his bedroom while he was masturbating. She would never tell him to "stop masturbating," and they would never talk openly about his masturbatory activities. Between the ages of twelve and fourteen he stole condoms from a drawer in the parental bedroom, condoms that belonged to his father, and put them on his penis and masturbated while thinking of making love to his mother. Sometimes when his parents were away he would lie on the parental bed and masturbate while looking at his mother's picture. At the same time, he would be petrified when his father returned home from work. He thought that his father would count his condoms and find out that some were missing and then be very angry and punish him.

When I learned more details about his childhood and his teen years I was reminded of a concept, "reaching up," that was first described by Bryce Boyer (1983, 1999) as a defense mechanism. "Reaching up" refers to a patient's excessive preoccupation with a conflict, its defenses and repetitions, and is associated with a particular level of childhood development that aims to escape a more anxiety-provoking conflict belonging to a lower-level childhood development. For example, a patient's constant and sometimes dramatic preoccupation with oedipal issues can be in the service of covering up a more hurtful pre-oedipal issue (see also: Volkan, 1995, 2010). Upon his return from his exile to Mexico, Manuel held on to his oedipal fantasies by reaching up.

Owing to her difficulties delivering her son, her relationship with and loss of her mother, being separated from her husband, and other possible reasons which I will never know, Manuel's mother would not help or even allow little Manuel to complete his separation-individuation and fully individuate. Under Manuel's "reaching up" there were unconscious murderous fantasies directed at his mother. In the second year of his analysis Manuel learned more about his mother sending him to another country and forcing him to live with people whom he did not know. Talking to his mother, he learned that just before the birth of his sister he had contracted a throat infection that had required a tonsillectomy, which had proved to be traumatic. His mother, then pregnant with the new baby, thought of Manuel as ailing, and she had sent him to his relatives in Mexico in the hope of "improving his health." The tonsillectomy was not the only body invasion Manuel had undergone as a child. His mother had become concerned over a swelling in his testicles just a few months before his tonsils were removed. The doctor she had consulted about this had injected the child's testicles with some medication using a needle. Little Manuel's unconscious fantasy was that he was rejected and sent to a different country by his mother because he was damaged. His mother told him that when he returned from Mexico she noticed his tan and evident weight gain and no longer thought of him as damaged or ill. But the effects of the physical exile remained behind the resumed bond, which Manuel needed to hold on to with open incestuous wishes and activities in order to help deny the image of a rejecting mother, and also hide his unconscious wish to "murder" her. Recognition of what he was hiding would induce feelings of guilt and the fear of never finding a needed "good" mothering object. His unconscious fantasy related to these concerns.

One time Manuel had almost "actualized" his unconscious fantasy. When he became an adolescent, at the age of twelve, his father gave Manuel the gift of a rifle and demanded that the boy study gun safety rules. Soon after this, Manuel took the rifle into the family room to show it to friends. Resenting his mother's reference to this as dangerous, he said, "I know what I am doing," pointed his gun at her, and pulled the trigger, sending a bullet into the wall behind her. It seemed a miracle that he had not killed her. Without going into details, I briefly want to mention that when Manuel fought in a war zone as an adult, some of his thoughts about the death and destruction he witnessed were also linked to his childhood fantasies.

At one point in the first year of his analysis, local papers were full with accounts of a murder. A male university student had killed the parents of his girlfriend, stabbing them many times so that the mother was almost decapitated. Between his sessions at this time, Manuel exhausted himself by striking a punching bag, which I thought represented his mother's pregnant belly. Because she was pregnant she had sent her son into exile. Toward the end of his first year of analysis Manuel came to a turning point when his associations to a dream allowed him to recognize and verbalize what was beneath his open incestuous behavior patterns. In his dream he was in a pigpen, but the pigs were bigger than him. Suddenly one of them, a dark one, reared up on its hind legs, pushed him and tried to bite him. Another pig, a light one, was lying down but he knew she was potentially more dangerous. Then he saw a weasel and he knew it was dangerous, too, and that he had to protect himself from it. He found a chair and used it, the way circus lion tamers do, to defend himself against attack from the weasel.

Manuel recalled that when he was ten years old, he had gone back to Mexico again, this time with his mother for a short visit. They had visited someone who kept huge pigs in a cage. He was told that pigs were dangerous and he felt frightened. He continued, "This is the same feeling sometimes I have in your office." He added, "These two pigs in my dream, one was mean and dark and the other was female and light. My father is dark, and my mother light. The male pig tried to bite me, but I had to be more careful of the female pig. I said to myself, 'Be aware of her!' The pigpen was like a gladiator's arena. One must fight to the death!"

I said, "I wonder who this weasel is? In the dream, you see your parents as dangerous. Could you consider that you are the weasel in order to protect yourself? But you don't like this weasel, you want to fight it. And this leads to a fight with yourself!"

He replied, "The weasel had a porcupine skin—sticks! Not to be beaten. There was a National Geographic show about weasels last night on television [day residue]. Of course, those on the TV were smaller than the one in my dream. But they were attacking a wolverine. Weasels are most vicious. Yes, it is disturbing to consider myself as sneaky, aggressive, and untrustworthy, but I have to do whatever is necessary in order to survive. It is a variation on my telling others, 'give me your best shot.'"

I replied, "It seems to me that the weasel needed to be born in you for protection. But note that in your dream you are aware of an inner struggle; you are fighting the weasel; you fight with yourself." Starting from his next session, Manuel stopped experiencing me as someone who would, at any time, send him into exile. I noticed his observing ego joining mine.

Manuel's case reminds us that everyone's childhood is filled with issues related to developmental issues, traumas from different times of life, fixations, mental defenses, sublimations, and adjustments to life. While working with refugees in the past, I have appreciated the efforts of organizations such as the United Nations High Commissioner for Refugees (UNHRC) to assist local helpers to settle refugees in new locations. However, due to the enormity of health problems during a refugee crises, UNHCR and other organizations deal with visible physical and mental issues including alcohol abuse and drug use. There are also diverse treatment options along with various legal, medical, and moral concerns (Wilson & Droždet, 2004). Under such situations there is difficulty in conducting in-depth studies of the minds of the refugees and their individualized psychologies. I present Manuel's case to illustrate that forced dislocation experiences may become intertwined with the newcomers' personalized psychological issues arising from their childhood, while they share common psychological responses, such as obligatory grief and mourning.

Reference to Manuel's immigrant family directs me to look at the fact that in the United States, besides direct descendants of Native Americans, everyone's family has a history of emigration. Often we notice that immigrants originating from the same country continue to live as neighbors at certain locations in America; this still happens now just as it has over the last century. Manuel's parents lived in a community of Mexican-Americans. I am familiar with places in Massachusetts where many families with a Finnish background are still neighbors. About thirty or forty years ago, these Finnish neighborhoods housed elderly first-generation immigrants who had never learned to speak English well, even though they had lived in the United States for many decades. Anthropologist Howard Stein (1980, 1993) has conducted extensive ethnographic fieldwork among multi-generation Slovak American and Rusyn American families, studying them and their larger cultural institutions in the Monongahela Valley in western Pennsylvania. He has described how immigrant Slovaks and Rusyns were stigmatized by second or third generation Americans who were anxious about their own social standing as real US citizens. Immigrant Slovaks and Rusyns first conducted life within a relatively circumscribed geographic community, which consisted largely of extended family, home, factory, church, fraternal organization, bar, and neighborhood. Over the second, third, and at the time of Stein's research, fourth generations, this tight local network had dissolved, at least outwardly, into the American "middle-class" ideal.

Paul Elovitz' and Charlotte Kahn's (1997) book on immigrant experiences presents detailed stories of immigrants from many countries and their similar mourning-adaptation processes. We learn about some immigrants' reasons for permanent dislocation, their issues related to cross-cultural marriages, and the impact of immigration on their children. The book also mentions famous Americans, ranging from Henry Kissinger to Arnold Schwarzenegger, who are immigrants themselves, and others, such as Colin Powell and Michael Dukakis, who are children of immigrant parents.

Nevertheless, data concerning details of an immigrant's, refugee's, or exiled person's internal world, and how dislocations become connected with various unconscious processes, are rare. Most of such data comes from biographies of psychoanalysts who are or were survivors of the Holocaust or offspring of survivors. In Chapter One I made references to Henri Parens' (2004), Anna Ornstein's (Ornstein & Goldman, 2004), Paul Ornstein's (Ornstein & Epstein, 2015), and Vera Muller-Paisner's (2005) books (see also Charlotte Kahn's 2008 memoir). I have already referred to the difficulties faced when conducting psychoanalytic psychotherapy with newcomer refugees and immigrants, mostly due to realistic practical obstacles in their acute situations, as well as their inducing certain emotions in the therapist. The best chance to observe the consolidation of different factors in creating specific behavior patterns or symptoms occurs when an individual is in psychoanalysis. I have never analyzed an adult refugee or immigrant during the acute state of their dislocation, and I am not aware of any publication describing such a psychoanalytic case.

CHAPTER FIVE

Living statues

This chapter describes another psychological factor that influences the internal world of a child immigrant's or refugee's internal world: parents may unconsciously "deposit" their traumatized self- and object images related to dislocation into the developing self-representation of their child and give him different tasks to deal with such images. Depositing is closely related to identification in childhood, but it is in some ways significantly different from identification. In identification, the child is the primary active partner in taking-in and assimilating an adult's images and owning that person's ego and superego functions. In depositing, the adult is the primary active person who plants specific images into the developing self-representation of the child. In other words, the child is used, mostly unconsciously, as a permanent reservoir for certain self- and other images belonging to the adult. The experiences that created these mental images in the adult are not accessible to the child. Yet, those mental images are pushed into the child, without the experiential/contextual framework that created them (Volkan, 1988, 2013, 2014c, 2015; Volkan, Ast & Greer, 2002). This type of transgenerational transmission, mixed with the children's or babies' own fantasies, will cause their new lives in a different country to take various directions. Memories of infants' own experiences in wars, war-like situations, and during forced migrations are not available to them when they are grown-up. The way that parents perceive and treat the infant during these traumatic conditions; the way they transmit their fear, anxiety, and other emotions to him; and the images they "put in" the infant's developing self-representation may casue the infant to evolve as a "living statue" (Volkan, 1979). I will relate here the stories of two such living statues.

Between 1968 and 1974 I was the director of the psychiatric service for adult inpatients at the University of Virginia Hospital. I came to know a bright twenty-seven-year-old Jewish graduate student who had been admitted to the hospital after a suicide attempt. During my interviews with him I noticed an unusual symptom: he wept *in silence*, although he was crying passionately, with tears coursing down his cheeks, an expression of great sadness on his face, and sobs convulsing him. No matter how intensely he threw himself into spells of weeping, it was always with this eerie soundlessness. Moreover, his crying would come to an abrupt stop and he would resume his conversation with me as though no interruption had occurred. When I called his attention to the sudden way in which he stopped his violent displays of emotion, he said that when he wept he had a sensation of having an iron hand tight around his neck, and that it was pressure from this hand that halted his crying.

The patient was born in 1943 to parents in hiding in Nazi-occupied Belgium. Although his parents were legally married, his mother, by denying that she was Jewish, managed to emerge from hiding and bear her infant in a hospital, even though this labeled the child as illegitimate. There were Jews employed in the hospital, and the mother asked that her child be circumcised. This request was probably a daring move for a Jewess to take in her determination to cling to her son's Jewish identity as well as her own, since it involved considerable danger under the circumstances. When she left the hospital she joined her husband in hiding, taking the baby with her. The infant's first seventeen months were spent in hiding, where he slept in a chest of drawers.

The boy's parents had originally come from Poland, which they had left before the Nazi invasion. The father had been caught by the Nazis before going into hiding, but he had escaped by jumping from the train on which he was being taken along with other Jews to a concentration camp. When the war was over and the couple and their child were living in safety, they sought word of relatives left behind in Poland.

They could learn nothing of their fate and concluded that they had been victims of the Nazi persecution.

Five years after their liberation, when the child was seven, the family migrated to New York, where the father, a tailor, hoped to prosper at his trade. He died when his son was thirteen, however, after having exhibited chronic depressive and tension states and being diagnosed with multiple sclerosis. When I saw the son as a patient years later, he told me that his mother remained in the apartment in which they had lived together as a family, and that she was determined to stay there even though the neighborhood had deteriorated and she had been mugged and beaten by marauding teenagers. It could be said that her tenacious adherence to the old neighborhood in the absence of any financial need to stay there indicated that psychologically she had never left the hiding place and continued to live in a physical and emotional prison.

Soon after her husband died the woman appeared on a television show giving an account of her family's terrible ordeal, which was designed to attract sympathy and financial aid, and she encouraged a similar beseeching attitude in her son, although he resented seeing it in himself when he came to recognize it. The boy was sent each summer "to camp" in order that he might "breathe fresh air." In this insistence, the wish for freedom was condensed with survival guilt in reference to those relatives and friends who had not escaped the concentration *camps*. Shortly after the father died, the mother abruptly terminated the Jewish mourning rites she had instituted and took her son to the countryside "for fresh air." While he was there, the boy caught a snake, which he put in a bottle of acid in order to watch its skin disintegrate. I suspected that this was an attempt to "kill" the father representation, with an unconscious wish to quickly terminate the process of mourning. He also identified with his father's mental representation in an unhealthy fashion, and developed "dermatological" problems himself for which he required lengthy treatment. He kept his father's broken camera, equipped with a "time delayer," as a linking object. The "time delayer" helped to postpone the mourning process. Its resemblance to a syringe also reminded him of the injections he had learned to give his dying father, during which he had fantasied "killing" him. Only much later, when he married a "Zionist woman," he was able to "breathe comfortably." He anticipated that she would protect him against the world and enable him to direct his aggression outwardly, and when he began to fear that he would lose her, he attempted suicide.

This patient's description of his early years in hiding was of great interest. I am sure that as an adult he was not able to recall events that occurred around him when he was a baby. Nevertheless, he would talk about how, "My mother salvaged strings of spinach from the garbage and made soup out of them," or, "We needed to bathe but there was no water and no soap." As he went on with particulars of their plight, he likened their experiences to those of Anne Frank. His memories were so lively that I had to keep reminding myself that this man had been but an infant during the time of hiding and could not possibly remember the events he described to me. It was evident that the parents had conveyed their memories to him. The child had been made a living repository of a tragic history so that it would never be forgotten. His identity as a human being was secondary to his identity as a living memento of Nazi persecution.

Through my work with him I uncovered the meaning of his unusual silent sobbing and his abrupt way of stopping his weeping under the pressure of an "iron hand" around his neck. It appeared that when the family was in hiding, the owner of the house made a practice of frightening the two Jewish families sheltered there by telling them that the Gestapo had arrived. This was a trick to obtain belongings from the Jews to sell, and only once did the Gestapo really come to the door. On this occasion the dog barked a warning. The infant who was to become my patient at the psychiatric inpatient unit was crying loudly, and those in hiding felt that he would give them away with his wailing and should be strangled for the safety of the group. His father set about choking him, but desisted and let his child "breathe" again when it was clear that the Gestapo had moved on. This pattern of strangling and choking a child to prevent him from crying out and betraying those in hiding to the Gestapo was observed by William Niederland (1961), who would also describe the "survivor syndrome" (Niederland, 1961, 1968). It is difficult to imagine the complexity of the patient's father's feelings as he found himself in this tragic situation. Again, the patient described this event as if he really remembered it. Family stories apparently stressed how the father had striven to rid himself of the guilt attached to this episode by repeatedly assuring his child as he was growing older that he would never have been surrendered alive to the merciless Nazis. External events involving aggression had shattered the life pattern of this family. They could do little about these events except create a special child as a memorial to their experiences and to the historical tragedy in which they had been caught up.

After the patient left the hospital he received psychoanalytic psychotherapy from one of my assistants under my supervision for a period of three years. The patient's outlook on life improved, his domestic problems lessened, and he was able to graduate from the university. However, his basic mission in life in the United States, his new country—to be a living repository of historical tragedy—remained and resisted attempts in his treatment to alter it. For example, I learned that whenever he was in a theater he would be overtaken by a hysterical blindness that made it impossible for him to see the exit signs. There was no exit for this man from his emotional hiding place nor any escape from the "illness" that was his core personality organization.

My assistant presented this patient's case at a psychiatric meeting held at the University of Virginia. The audience was, unsurprisingly, moved by the man's story, which I have summarized here. As the discussion of technical aspects of the psychoanalytic psychotherapy of the patient took place, several Jewish psychiatrists in the audience made an emotional plea that we *not* attempt to "cure" this man, since any cure would likely erase living testimony to history. I am indebted to Seymour Rabinowitz, my classmate when we were psychoanalytic candidates at the Washington Psychoanalytic Institute, for the term "living statue", with which he referred to this patient. At that time I did not know that I would meet another "living statue" in Cyprus.

The second "living statue" whose case I present to the reader here was still in his mother's womb when he fled to safety and became an internally displaced person. Obviously he had no memory of the trauma he and his mother experienced during this process. His name is Savaş, which in Turkish means "war." He was the son of a well-known Cypriot Turkish poet and novelist, whose work was widely read on the island as well as in Turkey. I first saw him in 1975 when I was granted permission from him and his father to report his story. I wrote about him couple of years later (Volkan, 1979). Since I could not conceal his identity, when I told his story I was not at liberty to provide details of his personal life or the story of his family. I limited myself mostly to what had become known about him publicly among the Cypriot Turkish community.

It is beyond the scope of this book to give a detailed history of Cyprus, so a general context must suffice. This Mediterranean island, known as the birthplace of Aphrodite, fell under the sway of one conqueror after another over the centuries, until its conquest by Ottoman Turks in 1570–1571, which introduced a cohesive and strong religious and cultural influence alongside the Hellenic remnants that survived. The Ottoman administration lasted for 300 years, until 1878, when Great Britain took Cyprus "in trust" by treaty with the sultan, who was assured of protection against Russia in return. It was formally annexed by the British in 1914 at the start of World War I, in which the Ottoman Empire allied itself with Imperial Germany. Cyprus became an independent republic in 1960. At that time, two ethnic groups on the island, Greeks and Turks, had been living side by side for almost 400 years. The Republic of Cyprus did not bring these two groups together, and ethnic conflicts began. On 21 December, 1963 violence erupted in the capital city, Nicosia. Turks would call this outbreak and the events of the following days the "Bloody Christmas Massacre." After many tragedies, the Turkish army came to the island in 1974 and divided it into north Cypriot Turkish and south Cypriot Greek sections. Peace negotiations between the two sides are still ongoing.

Six months after the island was divided, in the spring of 1975, I was in the northern part of the island when Savaş' father asked me to see his son professionally. At that time Savaş was a bright eleven-year-old boy, whom I liked on sight. His opening remark to me on our first meeting was that books are usually written only about famous people who are no longer alive, like Kemal Atatürk, but that one had already been written about him. I immediately felt that he was referring to himself as having been immortalized.

On 25 December, during the Bloody Christmas mentioned above, the well-known Cypriot Turkish poet left the mixed village where he lived and went to the Turkish section of Nicosia, the capital city. His wife and mother were to join him later. However, the two women were unable to escape to safety because their acquaintances, and even former friends, the Greeks in the same village, had suddenly become their enemies. They betrayed the women and the two were subsequently captured by Cypriot Greeks. On the first night of captivity the poet's wife gave birth to a son in the Nicosia General Hospital, which was then under Cypriot Greek control. The newborn child was left in a crib with other Cypriot Turkish infants who happened to be there at that time. However, the room they were placed in was also being used as a morgue for Cypriot Turkish casualties. A British nurse, shocked at this situation, managed to separate the living infants from the dead Cypriot Turks. The poet did not know for some time whether his wife and mother had survived their capture, but they were reunited on 10 January, along with the newborn baby, who was named "War" because of the circumstances of his birth.

Between 13 January and 10 March the poet wrote a series of poems addressed to his son. They were published under the title *Oğlum Savaş'a Mektuplar* (*Letters to My Son Savaş*) (Yaşın, 1965) and widely read by Cypriot Turks who were, at that time, living in fear. *Letters* begins with a description of the events taking place at the time the infant "was opening his eyes on the world," and the verse conveys a sense that this child was an immortal—or at least a very special—being:

> With a bullet from a lowly person
> You could have died, Savaş,
> Before you were born:
> You would die in your mother's belly
> Without getting to know
> The miracle called life
> Thanks to which you are saved.
> You were born ... .
> You might not have been born. (Yaşın, 1965, p. 18)

Each of the poems, most of which begin with a salutation like "Listen well, my son Savaş," clearly indicate that this is a child of destiny, a child who drew in the stink of death with his first breath. The volume concludes with a poem about "those who returned and those who did not." It tells the story of the day the Red Cross returned the Cypriot Turks captured during Bloody Christmas to the Turkish section. It is a moving poem, written from the viewpoint of the poet in the crowd anticipating the arrival of the Red Cross vehicles, sharing the anguish of those waiting for their lost ones. The poet is helpless and hopeless as he waits. The poem ends with his turning to the statue of Kemal Atatürk on the square where the crowd has gathered. In the poet's mind he sees tears in the eyes of the statue, and with his poet's ears he hears it say:

> If I were alive, my children,
> I would expunge your trouble. (p. 171)

It is clear that the parental perception of Savaş as a symbol of Bloody Christmas was later deposited in the boy's self-representation. When I began meeting with him I was struck by one of his symptoms. He had an odd sensation in the skin of his face; it felt dry, and he thought that if he scratched it, parts of his countenance would chip off as though it were the face of a stone statue. Connecting this symptom with Savaş' first statement to me, as well as with the final poem in his father's book, made me think that the image of Atatürk's statue was also deposited in Savaş.

Although he had carried the burden of being a special symbol of a war for as long as he could remember, Savaş became symptomatic during the 1974 Turkish military operation, when a stray bullet passed over his head as he sat in his room. This event inflamed in him the self-concept of having been close to death and saved by a "miracle", which was formed when his mother and grandmother had planned to escape to safety. His new narrow escape from a bullet strengthened the Atatürk image—at least the image of the Turkish leader's statue—within him. Young Savaş, like many Turkish children of those days, knew the story of the Turkish national hero's escape from death during the Gallipoli campaign, when shrapnel had hit his chest, shattering a watch in his breast pocket instead of killing him.

During the 1974 war Cypriot Greeks had to flee to the south of the island, leaving their homes behind. Soon after the war Savaş' family was given a former Cypriot Greek house in a town where a battle had been bitterly fought. When they took occupancy they discovered dead bodies still lying in the beautiful orange grove nearby, and the child learned the stink of death. This experience reactivated in his mind the lines his father had written about his being an infant whose first breath of life bore the taint of the decaying dead around him. Once more what was deposited in his self-concept dominated his mind. He was determined to be perfect to meet the expectations of his father and those his father reached with his stirring poetry. He became obsessively perfectionist in many little ways, avoiding cracks on sidewalks, insisting that when he turned on a water faucet the stream be precisely centered. After my short visit to the island, Savaş received help from a child psychiatrist. During my next visit to north Cyprus in 1977, the boy excitedly sought me out. I was delighted to find him without symptoms, although it was clear that he still regarded himself as destiny's child. Later he sent several letters to me in the United States, but as decades past, and Savaş and other members of his family moved from Cyprus, I lost contact with him.

After retirement from the University of Virginia Medical School in 2002 I began to spend the summer months in North Cyprus and learned that Savaş lived in England. Years later, during the summer of 2014, when I was walking in a district of the Turkish Cypriot side of divided Nicosia where there are many shops, a friend informed me that a new electronics shop had opened. He told me that Savaş had returned to the island, and that this shop belonged to him. I quickly went to this place and there, sitting behind a desk, I saw a man whom I could not recognize. He recognized me right away, however, and with great excitement hugged me. This moment, I am sure, will stay alive in my mind for the rest of my life. Soon, a beautiful woman walked in. She was Savaş' sister. She was born a few years after Savaş' dramatic birth experience and the poet and his wife had named her Barış (Peace). We took a picture of us that day in the store: War standing on my right and Peace standing on my left. Now each time I look at this picture it reminds me of the complexity of human nature and how many refugees, in their internal worlds, carry historical images of the struggle between humans' "bad" and "good" aspects, between War and Peace.

CHAPTER SIX

Double mourning: adolescents as immigrants or refugees

A nna Freud (1958), Erik Erikson (1963), Peter Blos (1968, 1979), and other psychoanalysts have described how the adolescence passage, the period of life between childhood and adulthood, is dominated by alternating regressive and progressive movements related to disengagement from early object images. Adolescents exhibit various observable behavior patterns, such as devaluing parents while idealizing a movie star or a peer group, rebelling against authority while searching for and submitting to a self-chosen leader, seeking quick success, and demonstrating quick frustration. They are also preoccupied with gender differentiation. Under these observable behavior patterns they are involved in many battles of earlier years. As Erik Erikson (1963) stated, after these battles, this period of turmoil ends with the consolidation of the individual's identity; or in Peter Blos' (1968, 1979) term, *a second individuation* occurs.

Martha Wolfenstein (1966, 1969) argued that the "normal" adolescent passage provides a *model* for an adult type of mourning. Youngsters learn how to modify or even let go of childhood images and change, to one extent or another, mental representations of others who were subjects of their childhood attachments and other types of intense relationships. Since immigration, especially forced immigration, also presents losses and gains, dislocation from a familiar place to a foreign one leads to youngsters combining their internal and external turmoil; they face what Amsterdam-based psychoanalyst Jelly van Essen has called, "double mourning" (Van Essen, 1999, p. 30).

As adolescents leave their homeland and move to a new country, they are also leaving their childhood and moving to adulthood. When they come to treatment, the therapist observes that these young people share certain fantasies and utilize certain psychological defense mechanisms. León and Rebecca Grinberg have described such youngsters' shared unconscious fantasies about their parents when emigration is voluntary: "The mother, in the boy's unconscious fantasy, emigrates to follow the father and does not consider the harm it may cause the child; the father, in the girl's unconscious fantasy, emigrates to offer secure or well-being to the mother without considering the girl's suffering" (Grinberg & Grinberg, 1989, p. 125). These fantasies reflect how these youngsters' review of their childhood oedipal issues during their adolescent passage becomes reflected in their perception of the reason for the family's voluntary move from one country to another one. In the late 1990s, Jelly van Essen (1999) worked with minors coming to the Netherlands from the Far and Middle East, Africa, Bosnia, Croatia, and Kosovo under traumatic conditions and observed that adolescents usually exhibit ambivalence about psychiatric treatment; seeking help can trigger helplessness and loss of control and foster regression or evoke aggression. She noted that many adolescents did not start therapy out of fear of being confronted with memories that they may not be able to handle, although these same intrusive recollections initially caused them to seek help. Once in therapy, Van Essen's adolescent patients used splitting as their main defense against uncertainties in the outer world, causing the young refugees to experience persons and countries as wholly "good" or "bad." For example, Van Essen's patient Kuno, age fourteen, appeared to have placed a wall between his previous and present life; but there were holes in this wall. For example, when his application for a residency permit was being processed by the Ministry of Justice, the young man could not fully maintain his splitting defense, and he experienced suicidal depression. Kuno was in once-a-week therapy for two years. The improvement in his emotional health followed a series of bizarre dream collages. In his repeating dreams, Kuno would attempt to integrate split or fragmented aspects of these images. These dreams reflected the patient's new ability to integrate what he had left behind and what he found in the new country, an integration of his internal world as a bicultural being. Van Essen described how difficult it was to conduct psychotherapy with adolescents like Kuno. Because of external realities, the therapist had to cooperate with a legal guardian, a lawyer, and school authorities, and consider safety issues.

Annette Streeck-Fischer's (2015) three adolescent cases from the present day illustrate how cultural and historical elements played a prominent role in the young people's difficulty in adjusting to life in Germany and in their consolidating identity formations. All three patients were more or less proficient in German, and Streeck-Fischer experienced no difficulty communicating with them. She emphasizes how the ethnic origin of an adolescent plays an important role "in the transgenerational transfer of cultural ideals, especially if the immigrant adolescent feels rejected by the new society and its culture" (p. 441).

The first patient was the fifteen-year-old son of a Polish-German mother and a Turkish father, both of whom had come to Germany as adolescents. The teenager's maladjustment to being an immigrant included his glorification of militant ideologies of his father's native country. The second patient was one year older than the first; she had lived in Moscow with her parents until she was eleven years old and experienced increasing anti-Semitism there. Through her symptoms and actions in a hospital setting, she managed to make her carers feel as if they were Nazi torturers or concentration camp guards. The third patient, fifteen and a half years old, was the daughter of a German mother and a black African father. In her case, boundaries between the mother's and the father's cultures were blurred, creating severe confusion and difficulty in reality testing. In these three cases we can easily see aspects of identification and depositing with associated fantasies, complicating the adolescent passage.

With the expansion of communication technology, many social networks have developed. Adolescents from different locations in the world learn more about the Other in foreign countries, but this situation also exposes them to conflicted orientations and values (Jensen, Arnett & McKenzie, 2011). When they experience a "double mourning" by becoming immigrants or refugees, they also become busy with images of different cultures and histories, and struggle to find a place in-between or tenaciously hold on to specific aspects of their culture or history.

CHAPTER SEVEN

A refugee family's story

Refugees struggle with attempts to integrate the images of what was left behind with what they face in their new environment. The nature and severity of other traumas they go through before, during, and following their dislocations are also inflamed and complicated by legal, cultural, religious, political, and medical issues, as well as security concerns. When there is a flood of refugees to a place, local authorities, as well as helpers from international organizations, become busy with immediate, practical matters. Tackling such matters does not leave time for *in-depth* investigations of refugees' internal worlds. Finding the newcomers bread to eat, clothes to wear, and a safe place to sleep supersedes considerations for psychological care, especially individualized in-depth psychological care. When there are organizations in the host country offering psychiatrists, psychologists, and other mental health professionals—very seldom psychoanalysts—to consult and treat refugees, only lucky ones like Kuno receive long-term psychotherapy. As I described in the last chapter, Jelly van Essen has explained some of the reasons why conducting psychotherapy with refugees is difficult. Here we should also remember the language issue. The newcomer is unlikely to speak the therapist's language and the therapist will have to use an interpreter. The presence of an interpreter translating another refugee's words to a foreign therapist will influence the patient–therapist interactions—especially when the interpreter has also likely been a refugee, with all the difficulties that entails. The therapist's human responses, ranging from experiencing intense empathy for the refugee, to witnessing human cruelty, to feeling helpless, may make it difficult for the therapist to hold on to her therapeutic identity.

After working in Cyprus, Tunisia, Georgia, Albania, Croatia, and elsewhere with dislocated persons, I came to the conclusion that the adjustment we see in refugees following big disasters usually points to their becoming perennial mourners, with both regressive and progressive possibilities. Different events in my life have resulted in my traveling to many locations in the world and participating, as a psychoanalyst, in unofficial political dialogues and peace-building activities. While I was visiting the Republic of Georgia I met an internally displaced family, and then, from 1998 to 2002, I visited them every four to six months. Each time I spent many hours with them as a "participant observer," to use Harry Stack Sullivan's (1962) term, in an effort to understand the family members' internal worlds. Either Manana Gabashvili or Jana Javakhishvili, both Georgian psychologists with perfect English, accompanied me during my visits to this family. As interpreters they became, in a sense, my extension. Sometimes I spoke with family members individually and conducted interviews the way I would undertake the psychoanalytic diagnosis of a patient. I investigated my subjects' fantasies and dreams, and especially tried to understand how they were reacting internally to changing external world events. This is the only refugee family that I have worked with so intensively. I report this family's story here, as even though events in their lives go back many years, their experiences, I believe, mirror those of refugees who are in similar situations today. For psychoanalysts who also work outside of their offices, for every mental health worker, and for anyone who is interested in the psychodynamic issues that arise in a family's adjustment to a new life in a new location after major trauma , this family, I believe, provides a good sample for examination and learning (Volkan, 2002, 2003b, 2006).

When the Soviet Union collapsed in 1991 and the Republic of Georgia declared its independence, brutal conflicts erupted between Georgians and Abkhazians, Georgians and South Ossetians, and even among Georgians themselves. Georgia then had a population of six million people. After the conflicts, 300,000 became internally displaced persons

(IDIs), who were in fact refugees in their own country. Of these, 3,000 Georgian refugees from Abkhazia were housed at Tbilisi Sea, starting seven years prior to my first visit to this place. Established as a holiday resort during the days of Soviet communism, Tbilisi Sea consisted of three luxury hotels surrounded by a man-made lake.

The family I went on to work with had originally lived in Gagra, on the northeast coast of the Black Sea. During the Soviet period, ethnic Georgians had also lived in Abkhazia. When the Georgian–Abkhazian war broke out and ethnic cleansing of Georgians in Abkhazia began, the family fled to Tbilisi, the capital of the Republic of Georgia. The local Georgians' sentiments toward IDPs were that "refugees should go home." Georgians belong to various tribes, and Georgians living in Abkhazia before the ethnic cleansing belonged to a special one. This, I think, was a factor causing many Georgians in Tbilisi not to welcome the newcomers. Even people from the same ethnic background can respond unfavorably to a flood of newcomers.

The family was settled at Okros Satsmisi (Golden Fleece), one of the hotels at Tbilisi Sea. When I first visited in May 1998, the former luxury hotel looked as if it had been hit by a devastating tornado: walls had been demolished, windows were covered with plywood or plastic sheets, stairways had become treacherous to climb, paint had long gone, hallways were cluttered with junk and dirt. IDP children only attended a nearby school in the late afternoon, after the local Georgian children had gone home. Some IDPs had become beggars due to their poverty.

How can a psychoanalyst help 300,000 persons living in misery in a location that resembles a huge garbage dump? How and from what point does one start a therapeutic process? Why did I choose to work with this family? When my team and I were involved in conducting unofficial dialogues between enemy representatives, we would suddenly, and often unexpectedly, notice an opportunity for a project that would attract the opposing parties' cooperation; we named such opportunities "entry points." During my first visit to Tbilisi Sea there was a crowd in front of Okros Satsmisi. A man who was introduced to me as Mamuka was dressed in paramilitary uniform. He was setting out with younger IDPs to take part in a "mini-war" with the Abkhazians. They were getting ready to get into old cars and trucks and drive to the Gali region of Abkhazia at the Georgian–Abkhazian border. I understood that now and then these migrants would fight with Abkhazians as guerrillas, under the illusion they would get back what they had left behind. Ooccasionally some of them would be killed in these "mini-wars." I was told that an anxious woman in the crowd was Mamuka's wife, Dali. When I spoke with her she told me that her anxiety was due to her older son's decision to join his father and others to go the Abkhazian front. I heard that there was only one working telephone in the three former luxury hotels, which were now crowded with 300,000 IDPs, and that this telephone was at Mamuka's "apartment" at Okros Satsmisi. I recognized that this family was seen as the leader by other IDPs, and decided that my "entry point" for dealing with all the refugees at Tbilisi Sea was to start working with Mamuka's family.

The family lived in the two former suites on the sixth and seventh floors of Okros Satsmisi. Each suite had a bedroom separated by a cloth curtain from a sitting area and a very small kitchen. In the bedroom there was a mattress on the floor and in the sitting room there was an old cot and three chairs. The members of the family consisted of Mamuka, Dali, their two sons (one twenty-one years old and the other eighteen), a daughter who was sixteen, and Dali's mother and father. The older couple lived on the seventh floor and the younger couple lived on the sixth floor in the same corner of the hotel. The children sometimes slept in their parents' "apartment," and other times at their grandparents' "apartment." The old yellow telephone was placed in front of the wall on a wooden table facing the entrance door of the younger couple's suite. When I first saw it I had a feeling that I was looking at a small statue of Jesus. The yellow telephone was placed on a clean embroidered cloth as if it was a most special and valued item. It was the only item to connect 300,000 people with the world outside their community in the case of an emergency. I learned that on occasion some of the refugees used this telephone when trying to receive information about family members and friends left behind in Abkhazia.

One of the suites had a balcony overlooking the lake, but I noted that there was no room to sit and enjoy the scenery as the family had piled their collected junk on the terrace. I have observed increased orality as well as anality among traumatized societies. Piles of objects such as empty breakfast boxes, torn clothes, or machinery parts that would never be used were everywhere at Tbilisi Sea. It was hard to walk through the hallways of Okros Satsmisi. I thought that such seemingly useless collections reflected what psychoanalysts call "orality": to collect things to "eat" so as not to notice being "hungry." At Tbilisi Sea people's orality was also condensed with their anal expressions to dirty the environment. Even though the materials collected by members of a traumatized community may sometimes be useful, the aim is to clutter their environment as though they live in an "anal" field of garbage (see also Šebek, 1992). They regress not only to oral preoccupations, but also turn their anal sadism against the area in which they live. I do not mean to minimize the reality of their lack of means to clean up and protect their environment; I am simply focusing on the psychological aspects of such behavior patterns. I recognized that Mamuka's family, as well as other refugees at Tbilisi Sea, needed to move up internally from oral and anal regression, and relibidinalize their self-esteem.

In Gagra, Mamuka had been a policeman and also a well-known soccer star. Dali was a teacher. Dali's father, Nodar Khundadze, was a well-known novelist and poet, and Dali was his only daughter. After ethnic conflict broke out in 1992, Mamuka left to join other local Georgians to fight Abkhazians. Later, knowing that his family and others were in danger, he arranged for a young Ukrainian helicopter pilot whom he knew to fly into the soccer stadium to take his wife and children to safety to Sukhumi, the capital of Abkhazia. In Sukhumi, help was available to take the fleeing Georgians to safety in Tbilisi. Dali and her children had only fifteen minutes to prepare for their departure; she did not even have time to take her jewelry. While running to board the helicopter, Dali and her children saw dead bodies and immense destruction. When the helicopter went back to rescue more Georgians, it was shot down, killing its young Ukrainian pilot. Eventually all the family members, including Dali's parents, were united at Tbilisi Sea. Their dog, Charlie, was left behind.

When I first briefly talked with Dali, as Mamuka was getting ready for the "mini-war", she told me: "So many people got killed, thank God we are alive." I learned that the family had been living at Okros Satsmisi for six years. I met and spoke with her again two days later, and a third interview took place after her husband returned. She was a very intelligent woman. She was also psychologically minded. While Mamuka was away, she dreamed that someone else's husband was killed and his widow was in grief. When she reported this dream to me, she realized that she was projecting her own possible predicament onto others.

The family was exhibiting various signs of perennial mourning. Even though each mini-war re-traumatized the family, Mamuka's returns to the Gali region for mini-wars maintained their belief that the

Georgians would recapture this region and then they would continue advancing all the way to Gagra. They did not accept the loss of their land. "We have a wound that will remain open forever," Dali told me. She recounted that on 20 September, 1992, as she and her children were rushing toward the helicopter, she carried her personal identity card, her Soviet "internal passport." During Soviet times, citizens had "internal passports" on which the individuals' ethnic identities were written. Dali's internal passport had her husband's name on it. It was well-known that Mamuka, the famous soccer player, had married the daughter of Nodar Khundadze, himself a well-known figure, a writer and a nationalist. Nodar had written against the Abkhazian treatment of Georgians, and he and his wife were in hiding and also trying to escape from Gagra. As Dali was running to the helicopter, she reasoned that if the helicopter had to land in enemy territory and if she and her children were caught, the Abkhazian captors would know from her identity card who she was. She was afraid that she could be forced to reveal her parent's whereabouts. Thus, on an impulse, Dali ran back to her house and left her internal passport there before returning to the helicopter and safety. Eventually she arrived in Tbilisi, and later traveled to Tbilisi Sea, without an identity card, a document that had also indicated, she emphasized to me, her birthplace. She was a "daughter of Gagra."

By coincidence, after escaping from Gagra, Dali had seen on Russian television, while in Tbilisi, the beloved home they had left behind going up in flames. Even though she knew that the house was badly damaged or burned down, she held on to the illusion that her original identity card still existed in Gagra. As an IDP, Dali was eligible to apply for assistance from authorities in Tbilisi and by doing so would receive about five dollars per month to support herself or her family members. I must add here that at that time five dollars was a far more substantial sum for the IDPs than it might appear to outsiders. What seemed odd on the surface was the fact that Dali was refusing to do what was necessary to receive this money: she would not obtain a new identity card from the Georgian authorities. Yet every night she would have a hard time falling asleep as she wondered how to feed her children and husband. Dali seemed to be "paralyzed" and unable to take action to secure the much-needed funds. For her, it was more important to cling to her identity as a Georgian from Abkhazia than receiving the needed money. I clearly understood that her "symptom" was an indication of her perennial mourning. The whole family also shared a "living linking object" in a dog, another indication of their being stuck in perennial mourning.

While Dali was watching their home in flames on a Russian television she thought that she caught a glimpse of their dog Charlie. She became determined to know Charlie's fate. Through considerable effort, the family eventually learned that Charlie had been hit by a car and killed. During their second year at Tbilisi Sea, Dali and her children found a black dog roaming among the garbage at Tbilisi Sea and thought it looked like Charlie. They adopted the new dog and named him "Charlie." Everyone in the family was conscious of his psychological significance. Through the new Charlie, the old Charlie was "reincarnated," and the illusion of bringing the images of lost objects—dead relatives, friends, home, Gagra—back, psychologically speaking, was possible. I still remember the second Charlie very well; he would lie under Dali's feet as if he had priority for the best place in this small "apartment."

I was very surprised when I found another poet, like Savaş' father in Cyprus, who wrote poems to describe his family's and other internally displaced Georgians' conditions. When we sit in our comfortable homes far away from refugee camps and see pictures of people living in horrible conditions on television or in newspapers, we do not think that some of these severely traumatized people had been shining stars in their original communities. Dali's father Nodar was such a person. Now, as a refugee on the seventh floor of Okros Satsmisi, every night he would write a poem. The next morning when the whole family got together on the sixth floor for breakfast, Nodar would read his previous day's poem. It was Dali's duty to file her fathers' poems and protect them in her apartment. Poems were the family's precious linking phenomena.

The following poem, titled "Children beggars," is an example of Nodar's description of conditions and emotions, oral needs and helplessness of his and his fellow IDPs at Tbilisi Sea.

> When I see your hand begging
> My dignity suffers.
> I cannot give you my soul (suli)
> Since it is impossible to give one's soul to someone.
> But, I have nothing left but my soul.
> I am pressing against prison bars

If you need my life,
I can give it to you.

An agreement between the Georgian government and the Abkhazians to stop mini-wars shattered the refugees' illusions that they would win back their land and the families would return home. Nodar's anger at the Georgian government is clearly expressed in the following poem:

I feel there is betrayal in my motherland
Dishonesty wins
I am leaving all that I have here
And I am coming to you, the sun.
Everything around me is in darkness
I do not see a thing
A snake is biting me bitterly
And, is achieving its betraying aim.
We could not realize what was happening
Everything appeared to be confused
But, I know the enemy is in Tbilisi
Oh! Oh! Let my enemy's life to be short.
I see my motherland's suffering from betrayal
Oh, the devil wins
Depression conquers my soul
I pray you, the sun, help us

The above poems were translated into English by Manana Gabashvili. During my visits to Tbilisi Sea Manana or Jana Javakhishvili and I would spend several hours at the Mamuka family's "apartment," watching them carry out some of their usual daily activities, such as Dali cooking, the children getting ready to go to their schools, or Mamuka, who had obtained second-class police work in Tbilisi, returning from work. Dali was my primary source of information about the family, and I would conduct long interviews with her. Sometimes she would take Charlie out of the hotel and my interpreter and I would accompany her. Along the way, I would also talk with refugee children. Others at Okros Satsmisi, and I suspect many at Tbilisi Sea, knew that a psychiatrist from America visited Mamuka's family every four or six months and talked with Dali about life at this place. Dali would be informed of my visits some months or weeks in advance. No other adult outside of the

Mamuka family asked to speak with me, but I learned that, early on, Dali had started to meet regularly with a group of ladies from Tbilisi Sea after my visits. She would share with them what she and I had talked about and what insights she had gained from such talks. It was as if she had started her own "group therapy" sessions. Talking with Dali I realized that I was perceived by her and her friends as a "libidinalizing new object" from America. I would not give her advice to do this or that. I was also very careful not to embarrass the family by bringing gifts. If I had, their culture would force them to give me gifts in turn, and they could not afford to do so. Instead I would collect pencils, papers, or key chains from exhibits at psychiatric and other medical meetings and carry them with me to Dali, who would later give them to the refugee kids at Tbilisi Sea.

Soon after my work started, Dali began dreaming about me. I appeared most often in her dreams in an undisguised fashion when she had been informed of my visits by our Georgian contacts. Dali was not my analysand, and I could not fully understand her dreams without the benefit of a workable transference neurosis within the frame of an analytic setting. Nevertheless, the manifest content of her dreams was sufficient to suggest the nature of her transference to me. Whilst in the initial dreams I brought her goods to satisfy her oral needs or accompanied her in creating explosions (anal sadism), she later began to dream of me (still undisguised) as someone sleeping next to her and her husband. She was embarrassed to tell me this. I sensed that she would try to move up from oral and anal preoccupations to higher-level psychosexual interests. Her daughter, Tamuna, exhibited the same pattern in her dreams. Tamuna's dreams slowly changed from my bringing her food to my bringing her a baby.

Referring to her dreams, Dali said that as it would not be proper for me to sleep with her and Mamuka, the family should do something else. So, in 1999, they began to build a room for me. They walled off a section of the hallway in front of their "apartment" and started turning it into a living space. They called it "our Vamık's room." While the room was being built and furnished they would not allow me to enter it. It took more than a year for them to complete this project, which, of course, the Tbilisi Sea community was aware of. From a psychoanalytic point of view, the Mamuka family was involved in a "therapeutic play" (Volkan, 2010, 2015); by making a change in their external lives they were preparing to make a change in their internal worlds. I agree with Peter

Neubauer (1993) that play can be an attempt at a solution for conflict, of the establishment of ego mastery. As the family "played" together, as they constructed their new room and named it "our Vamık's room," my mental image was with them when I was not physically present.

As the room project was underway, Nodar continued to share his poems with the family every morning and Dali continued to file them in a special place. While talking with me, she indicated that she understood that her father's poems were concrete symbols of the loss of their former lives, as well as their hope to return home. Their pre-refugee identities and refugee identities were linked, but as they could not commit themselves fully to either identity, they remained in an indeterminate state. With this insight there was a change in Dali. A year after I started to work with her she went to Tbilisi and obtained a new identity card. This was a sign that she and her family were doing some work of mourning, and Dali was able to invest in a new object protecting her self-esteem. However, perennial mourning was still present. When I had first met them, the family were making plans to return to Gagra within three years, even though six years had passed since they had become refugees. Now they began to speak of a five-year plan.

During my first visit to Tbilisi in 2000 my Georgian friends told me that Dali was ill. She had lost weight and had withdrawn from her environment. Apparently a Georgian physician had diagnosed her condition as a cerebral stroke. I was shocked and arranged to go to Tbilisi Sea the next day with Jana. Dali was lying on the old cot in the sitting room, looking like a ghost. I asked other members of the family to leave me, and of course Jana, alone with Dali. After they left I spent over an hour talking with Dali who seemed to be very depressed and suicidal. It did not take much time to realize what had caused her to give up her adaptation to daily life as a perennial mourner and develop "melancholia." As the completion of "our Vamık's room" was taking place, the second Charlie had died from natural causes. I interpreted the meaning of Charlie's death to her. I explained that without her living linking object, she could no longer remain a perennial mourner; the realization of her loss was now hitting her very hard. She was feeling guilty for leaving the first Charlie behind. I also noted her guilt feeling about the death of the Ukrainian helicopter pilot who had saved her and her children's lives. She wished that she or Mamuka could find a way to prevent him from going back to Gagra that final time. Dali's severe melancholia was complicated not only by the loss of the second Charlie and her recalling the death of the helicopter pilot, but, as I would learn soon, also by other factors.

Soon after the second Charlie's death, the Georgian Ministry of Internal Affairs organized a soccer match between local players from Tbilisi and IDP players from Abkhazia in memory of a Georgian player who had been tortured and killed by the Abkhazians. Mamuka scored two goals in the match. He was given a trophy inscribed with his name and the date of the match. Mamuka also became the commander of the Tbilisi and Tbilisi Sea police unit composed of IDPs from Tbilisi Sea. His new boss treated Mamuka with respect, restoring his self-esteem and verifying and extending his pre-refugee identity as a policeman in Gagra. He changed his five-year plan to return to Abkhazia to a ten-year plan, indicating further acceptance of the loss of his pre-refugee identity, his home, and Abkhazia in general. Meanwhile, Dali's two boys were attending college during the day. The boys began dating local young women who were also IDP's. They fell in love, and the eldest was married.

Dali's father also received verification of his continued identity as a literary figure. Nodar Khundadze's poems were published in book form in Georgian (Khundadze, 2000 [translated for this edition]) and recognized as an important piece of literature. He was given an award, and he was transformed by the experience. When he gave me a copy of his book, I noticed that this ever-angry man was now a man who often smiled. However, he told me how he and his wife were worried about their daughter's "cerebral stroke." (Incidentally, every time I visited the family on the sixth floor of Okros Satsimi, Dali's mother always stayed in her seventh-floor apartment. I never met her.) I told Nodar that Dali had not suffered from a cerebral stroke.

After his book was published, Nodar continued to write a poem each day. He would still ritualistically bring his poems to the breakfast table, but now only Dali would sit down and listen to him read. She continued to file the new poems, which still included references to the refugees' situations, but now Nodar would give the poem to Dali, smile, and leave the room. Dali found herself to be the only person in charge of the family's linking phenomenon; the others were developing new identities, in Salman Akhtar's (1999a, 1999b) term, going through a "third individuation." Dali felt alone.

Still another factor was contributing to Dali's severe depression. "Our Vamık's room" was nearing completion, and she had to face the reality that I was not a family member. Psychologically, it meant that she could not really possess me as an idealized "libidinalizing" new object, most likely as an "oedipal father."

During this trip to Georgia I visited Dali almost every day for a little over a week and discussed with her all the factors contributing to her melancholia. I told her that I could still care for her and her family even though I would not sleep in "our Vamık's room" after it was completed. She recognized that it was her responsibility to break or maintain the family's ties to the past. She also recognized that her "wish to get well," to "cut this bond" and "kill" the family's pre-refugee identity, was also causing her guilt.

Whenever I went to Tbilisi Sea I noticed that often there was a funeral. People Dali's age or even younger would drop dead, often for no apparent reason. I told Dali that there were other IDPs who were "killing" themselves, and added that, if she did not die, she could be a model for other IDPs as someone who could survive and make a good adjustment.

When I went back five months later, I did not recognize Dali. She had gained weight and was smiling. There was a new dog in the "apartment," a female named Linda. Dali told me that she was determined to avoid acquiring another "Charlie" as a living linking object. During this visit Mamuka, dressed in his best civilian clothes, wanted Dali to set up a table for us in "our Vamık's room," now decorated and furnished. Dali told me that she did not wish to break our tradition of meeting in the original sitting room, which had also been renovated. The new room, she said, was no longer "our Vamık's room;" it was theirs. The family members watched me enter the new room. I was amazed to see that it even had a fireplace. Mamuka's soccer trophy, given to him after the soccer match between local players and IDP players from Abkhazia, stood on the mantle. Mamuka wanted me to feel how solid and heavy it was. I sensed that the trophy symbolized his new post-refugee identity. Above the fireplace was a big painting of the Hotel Gagribsh, which had been the best-known location in Gagra when the family had lived there. Now it was in the former "our Vamık's room," like a tombstone that helps mourners bring their mourning process to a practical ending. The painting, framed, was not a linking object. They openly talked about how it symbolized the reality that there would be no return to Gagra. The family had given up their ten-year plan to go back. The painting was a "futureless memory" (Tähkä, 1993).

Mamuka discussed his last mission to Abkhazia in 1998. Now he explained how his thoughts of reconquering Gagra had been fanciful. "To harbor such wishes and dreams was senseless," he added. He described how he was much calmer, but still smoked heavily. His nightmares were gone. Perhaps as an expression of lingering, "silent" depression, he had difficulty in falling asleep, though he was "normal" by day.

My visit, during which I was taken into the former "our Vamık's room," followed the marriage of the family's youngest son. I was introduced to the new bride. There was an atmosphere of festivity, but Dali told me that the day after her youngest son got married she had experienced an anxiety attack and she wanted to understand why. So, she and I once more had a private conversation, with Jana as the interpreter. For a long time, before his marriage, her youngest son slept in the sitting room on the cot, separated from the parents' bedroom by a curtain. The oldest son and his wife had moved elsewhere after their marriage, and Tamuna was sleeping upstairs in her grandparents' "apartment." Dali woke up on the day after her youngest son's marriage, and came from her "bedroom" to find her son's cot empty. It was then that she had her anxiety attack. She knew that "separation" from her son would be difficult, but for some reason she also knew that her attack was connected to a sense that someone was going to die. She recalled how her children had cuddled around her in the helicopter, and she visualized herself as crying, feeling that she would die if she lost one of her children. She realized that seeing her son's empty cot had rekindled that fear, and it had overwhelmed her. Separation and a sense of actual death were connected in her mind.

For the first time, Dali informed me that the helicopter pilot who was killed had the same name as her son. She described the pilot, young and handsome, like her two sons. Not finding her son in the cot symbolized her guilt over being indirectly responsible for the young pilot's death, which Dali fully recognized. She told me that when the IDPs got together, the pilot's name would come up, but there was no memorial or public mourning for him. Our discussion ended with the idea that she could attend church and perform a funeral rite for the dead pilot, which could decrease her feelings of guilt and help her to separate her son(s) from him. A week later, Dali sent me a message to say that she had gone to church, lit candles for the dead pilot, prayed for his soul, and was feeling much better.

Once the Center for the Study of Mind and Human Interaction activities in Georgia and South Ossetia (Volkan, 2006) came to an end, we stopped traveling to these places, and the last time I saw Dali, Mamuka, and other members of the family was in March 2002. Dali looked radiant. During our last meeting she told me how proud she was of the family for building the new room. She added that they most likely would never make enough money to build a new home, but the room was a token of their triumph over the tragedy they had gone through. I congratulated her for no longer calling it "our Vamık's room." The yellow telephone was placed in a new, but renovated place. During the years I visited Mamuka and Dali's apartment I never heard it ring, and no one used it to make a call during my presence.

After March 2002 I continued to communicate with Georgian professionals with whom I worked closely (Volkan, 2013). Besides Manana Gabashvili and Jana Javakhishvili, others were aware of my work at Tbilisi Sea. They informed me that big changes had occurred at this place. I learned that Dali continued to meet with other IDP women and function as a "consultant" to them. Many IDPs "copied" Mamuka and Dali by building new rooms and cleaning their surroundings. I understood that funding from Norway had become available for them. They had turned Tbilisi Sea into a clean and livable settlement. The general consensus was that the number of people dropping dead for "no apparent reason" had decreased considerably. I was, however, given no scientific statistics on this subject. I wondered if Dali, by surviving her "stroke," had become a model for defeating depression, since many at Tbilisi Sea had been following her progress at the time. Tamuna managed to send me a short message in the mid-2000s, informing me that the family was doing well. At the end of the decade I was excited to be invited to a meeting in Tbilisi. I was sure that my hosts would find a way for me to visit the family during my short stay. Unfortunately, the day I arrived in Tbilisi, now a much changed city, I became ill with abdominal symptoms and a high fever. I spent my few days there in bed and had to leave Georgia without seeing Dali, Mamuka, or the other family members. I was most disappointed. I learned that Dali and Mamuka had become grandparents, and I was surprised to hear that Tamuna had become a nun. I had seen no evidence of deep religious preoccupations among the family members when I had met with them. I wondered whether the horrible trauma Tamuna had been through and the fact that she had spent her teen years as a refugee had played a role in her becoming a nun. I will never learn this.

As I conclude the moving story of this family I would like to make one last point. Although they suffered at the hands of Abkhazians, I do not wish to give the impression that Abkhazians are "bad" people. In this book I do not refer to historical events that were traumatic for Abkhazians. After spending decades visiting conflicted areas of the world I have come to the conclusion that people everywhere, along with their different cultural customs, religions, and history, are the same; they may collectively become involved in inhumane activities. Even when there is a division within the same ethnic group, people belonging to one ideology will hurt, molest, and kill people on the opposite side who belong to the aggressors' ethnic group. My latest examination of this type of situation occurred in the fall of 2015, when I participated in a meeting at El Bosque University in Bogota and spent time with Colombian psychoanalytic colleagues. My visit to Colombia took place when representatives of the Revolutionary Armed Forces of Colombia (FARC) and the Army of National Liberation (ELN) were reaching a peaceful agreement with the Colombian government representatives in Havana, Cuba. The FARC are Marxist-Leninist in their ideology and had been involved in kidnapping, ransom, extortion, illegal mining, and illegal drugs to fund their existence. The ELN is a lesser-known group in Colombia, which has also been involved in guerrilla activities associated with communist ideology. With its beginnings in 1964, the Colombian armed conflict is the longest-running armed conflict in the Western hemisphere. It has caused the death of more than 220,000 people, of whom eighty percent were civilians. Tens of thousands of Colombians have become refugees or immigrants in the United States, Spain, or other South American countries such as Ecuador and Venezuela. It is estimated that there are 50,000 Colombian refugees in Ecuador alone. According to the Associated Press (Frej, 2015), as the European refugee crisis was expanding, on 8 September, 2015 Venezuela's President Nicolas Maduro announced Venezuela was prepared to receive 20,000 Syrians "and share this land of peace." This humane gesture, however, took place when anti-Colombian xenophobia was rising in Venezuela, and about three weeks earlier, Venezuelan authorities had dispatched both police and National Guard troops to deport 1,400 Colombians living in Venezuela.

When I was in Colombia in 2015 I heard stories of refugees and farmers who had to move from their lands to other parts of Colombia when the FARC used their farms for illegal mining. In a sense, they too were IDPs. Dislocations were accompanied by horrifying tragedies. I met a lady whose niece's naked body had been thrown into a Bogota street by the guerrillas. The focus of my discussions in Colombia was how, once a final agreement is signed, to start physically bringing together in a peaceful fashion people from opposite sides who have been fighting for over sixty years. I was impressed that Colombian psychoanalysts had become seriously involved, with other professionals, in the effort to find answers to this question and consider possible "entry points." This work requires a close look at the psychology of how people develop prejudice about the Other who belong to another large-group identity, how collective prejudice evolves, and how it can become malignant. We should not deny, or hesitate to examine and try to understand, why human beings individually and collectively are capable of performing immoral, inhumane, and dreadful deeds.

PART II

HOSTS

CHAPTER EIGHT

Prejudice on a psychoanalytic couch

W e may all decry prejudice, but in truth we are all prejudiced—it is an element of who we are as human beings. It can be *benign*, *hostile*, or even *malignant* (Parens, 1979). In this book my focus is not on pairs of individualized sameness and difference, such as black and white, female and male, gay and straight, rich and poor, but rather on *us and them*. I focus on situations where tens of thousands, hundreds of thousands, or even millions of people *share* the same or similar prejudice against another large group and, keeping the theme of this book in mind, against newcomers. This kind of large-group prejudice can also be benign, hostile, or malignant.

In Part I, clinical findings and theoretical explanations on mourning and its complications were first presented in order to develop an understanding of the psychology of immigrants and refugees; the following chapters then looked at how immigrants and refugees cope with losing their original environment, people, and things, and their attempts to adjust to their new locations. In Part II, before I focus on people's reactions to newcomers, I will once more present clinical data. This time I will illustrate how we notice and explain the reasons for the appearance of prejudice in patients. I will present data from a patient who was not an immigrant or refugee. I will illustrate the reasons for his prejudice against his newcomer analyst who spoke English with an accent. When an individual's prejudice is observed while he is on an analytic couch, it can be examined under a psychoanalytic microscope and factors leading to such an attitude can be observed clearly. In the next chapter I will examine how prejudice about the Other who belongs to a different large-group identity evolves during developmental years and how shared prejudice is formed.

Hamilton was fifty-seven years old when he became my analysand many years ago. His analysis, from its beginning to its termination, has been described elsewhere (Volkan & Fowler, 2009b). The following are selected excerpts from his sessions during a one-and-a-half-week period at the end of the fourth year of his analysis.

Hamilton began one of his sessions by asking me a question: "Are you Jewish?" I said nothing. He knew that I was of Turkish origin, but now he decided that I might be a Turkish Jew. He made anti-Semitic remarks. Hamilton was a Christian and very proud of his Anglo-Saxon ancestors' history and their civic and religious accomplishments, but he was not a deeply religious person. Until then, throughout his analysis he had refrained from making unfavorable prejudicial statements about other ethnic groups even when, earlier in his analysis, he had become interested in Turkish history because of my background and had read some books on the subject.

The day that Hamilton asked me if I were Jewish was a Friday. I had just told him that I would not be able to see him on the Friday of the following week, but I could, however, meet with him on Tuesday instead. I saw him four times a week, and we did not have routine sessions on Tuesdays. Hamilton did not want to make up for the session that would be missed. It was not because it would be inconvenient for him to come on Tuesday; he simply did not think that he needed to come on that day. Uncharacteristically, he raised his voice like a stubborn child and refused my offer.

By the end of this session Hamilton and I understood the first meaning of his thinking of me as a devalued Jew. For some months prior to asking me if I were Jewish, Hamilton had been preoccupied with setting up a date for terminating his analysis. I had not responded to his tentative inquires. At this particular session he said that he had decided not to accept my offer of the replacement session in order to find out if he could experience a brief separation from me without experiencing anxiety. Rejecting my offer was in the service of his attempt to test his increasing autonomy and see if he truly could enter into the termination phase. When he became curious about turning me suddenly into a devalued Jewish person, he realized that this reflected his wish to continue depending on me, which would be the opposite of the expression of his independence from me. If I were a stingy Jewish person, as Hamilton indicated, I would not want to lose money and would demand that he make up for the missed session. Then he would obey me, still depend on and submit to his analyst/father, and would not be separated from me. In brief, his externalizing his stereotyped, unfavorable Jewish image on me and his exhibiting prejudice was related to his conflict and anxiety about entering or not entering the termination phase. He acknowledged that he wanted to finish his analysis, but he still felt "a lack of preparation."

During his next session with me on Monday, Hamilton continued to make anti-Semitic statements and speak of me as a devalued Jewish person. He connected his thinking with a kind of reality testing. In reality, on a bookshelf in front of my couch I exhibited some items I had collected during my travels to different countries. One of the displayed items was a gift from the then president of Ben-Gurion University in Israel. It was a triangular symbol of the university, with some Hebrew script designed to look like a flame. Hamilton thought that because this item was displayed prominently I might be Jewish. He also informed me that the Friday when his session was canceled would be a Jewish holiday.

Hamilton perceived the flame as a volcano (Volkan). In his mind, this item symbolically stood for my object representation. The Jewish alphabet looked "foreign" to him. Since he was thinking of terminating his analysis he wanted to talk about our "cultural and historical differences." He referred to the idea of his making only selective identifications with the analyst's images and functions. He wanted to separate from me without using aggression and without putting some unwanted elements into my image that would not then not be analyzed. This time his prejudicial remarks were connected with his re-experiencing individuation and autonomy.

After feeling pleased by noticing how he utilized prejudice as an aspect of a struggle for progression in his analysis, toward the end of this session Hamilton once more turned his attention to the Hebrew "volcano" and imagined me as an aggressive Jewish person who could punish him. This time he would be the devalued party. What he had externalized on me re-entered his self-representation. Hamilton's psychologically taking in what he had put out earlier led to his reviewing his childhood relationship with his sadistic father who often used to beat him. The father would put the little boy's head between his legs, pull the child's pants down, and hit the child's buttocks with a razor strap. By this time in his analysis Hamilton was very familiar with the influence of his father's relationship with him on his mental life. He went on to recall a Jewish boy from his high school years. The boy was the only Jew in the class. Having empathy for this young man, he thought that the young Jewish boy had felt isolated, just as Hamilton had felt isolated as a child in his peculiar home surroundings. He said that by thinking of me as a Jewish person, he might be displacing the image of himself as an abused child onto me. A new meaning for his prejudice came to light: it was linked to his attempt to get rid of his victimized aspects, deny them, and forget them permanently.

Hamilton did not come on Tuesday. On Wednesday he perceived the triangular Ben-Gurion University emblem as a detachable penis standing on my table. It was as if there was only one penis between the father and the son or between the analyst and the analysand. In his mind, he could steal it. Once more, he reviewed what he had "learned" in his analysis much earlier. Jewish men (as well as Turkish men) are circumcised/castrated, and he did not want a Jewish/Turkish penis. He had a conflict between wishing to take the father/analyst penis and be a man, and not wishing to take it since what was available to him might not be a proper penis and he might remain castrated. This time Hamilton's anti-Semitic remarks were connected with his conflict over completing his working through his oedipal issues.

On Thursday Hamilton reported a dream that he had had the previous night. In the dream he was in a bathroom with the president of the United States. When he described the president he used the word "seedy." The president took out his penis to urinate. My analysand, in the dream, thought that the president's penis was no different than his.

Hamilton was aware that the president represented his analyst, and went on to associate seediness with Jewishness. Once more he made unfavorable, unsubstantiated remarks about Jewish people and their religious customs such as circumcision. With my help he also understood that the dream reflected his wish to be a man, equal (symbolically in penis size) with his analyst/oedipal father. But he was worried that the Jewish/Turkish analyst's circumcised penis might not be good enough for his wished-for manhood. His unfavorable prejudice about Jewish people was once more linked with his oedipal transference story.

As arranged, we missed the next session which was on Friday. On Monday following this missed session Hamilton continued to make anti-Semitic statements. What came to his mind was the fact that Freud was Jewish. He kept saying that Freud had played around with his wife's sister. Hamilton was also aware that this thought was connected with his childhood games with a sister, which had made him feel guilty. This meaning of his prejudice was in the service of displaying and projecting guilt-inducing experiences and thoughts onto the Jewish Freud/analyst.

Hamilton came to his Wednesday session and reported that the day before he had uncharacteristically bought a lottery ticket. He felt like a child doing it, but he had a fantasy that he would win a great deal of money. Noticing his psychologically taking in what he had put in me earlier (money-crazy Jew), gave him an urgent need to understand why he had suddenly become a person contaminated with prejudicial thoughts linked with affects. Both of us were able to understand the deeper meaning of "money-crazy Jew" in his mind. When his father had physically abused him, little Hamilton had had fantasies of blasting his father with fecal material. Hamilton told me that he had been embarrassed while buying the lottery ticket. He understood that his fantasy of having a great deal of money was related to having a great deal of fecal material. We were able to work on this and re-examine how he had projected his anal sadism to me; how, when he took it back, he felt embarrassed; and how working through his anal sadism was connected with his wish and lack of preparedness for entering the termination phase of his analysis.

Hamilton recalled that a well-known country club in the city where we lived had begun accepting Jewish people (and African Americans) as members only in recent years. He reminded me that he would not apply for membership of this club because he had perceived them as racists and unfair to Jewish persons. The realization that he himself had hidden anti-Semitic thoughts made him feel guilt, shame, and remorse. He stated that before finishing his analysis he wanted to quickly disown unacceptable things about himself. He told me that his indulgence in prejudice was also in the service of individuation. "It is a mixed bag," he murmured, and added, "It may be harmless if one does not succumb to it." Then he told me that he would wonder how to end our psychoanalytic relationship gracefully. During the rest of his analysis he never made another anti-Semitic remark.

This case vignette illustrates an individual's various reasons, even though they may be linked, for expressing prejudice. Many individualized factors are present for other people who also feel and express prejudice. Since they are not in analysis, and since they join many others in xenophobic attitudes, they do not know, or at least they do not focus on, psychological issues that make them hold such attitudes. If there are realistic reasons, such as noticing some newcomers' jihadist involvement, many persons' prejudice will join together and collectively become crystallized as the "normal" thing to believe. Thus, human history illustrates the repeated appearance of anti-Semitism, Islamophobia, racism, neo-racism, apartheid, ethnic hatred, fascism, anti-Westernization, as well as ethnocentrism, and national or religious exceptionalism. These all refer to differentiations between large-group identities and arise from the wish to protect one's large-group identity from the Other's identity.

Hamilton's overt anti-Semitism was not sustained over a long period. It is important to note that he borrowed it from what existed, overtly and covertly, within the environment in which he lived. There are individuals who exhibit sustained prejudices—for example, against their neighbors—that belong only to them. Most observable sustained prejudices are shared ones and they are against Others who have a different ethnic, religious or ideological belief. During the one-and-half-week period in which he expressed anti-Semitic thoughts, Hamilton recalled his father's unfavorable preconceived irrational remarks about Jewish people and his business arrangements with them. He recalled how many persons from his childhood in a wealthy Protestant neighborhood in Virginia had made anti-Semitic remarks and frequent references to the prejudicial activities of the country club mentioned above. For personal, specific psychological reasons, during this week and a half of his analysis, Hamilton reached out and found a "shared" prejudice.

CHAPTER NINE

The Other

B efore focusing on prejudice against refugees and immigrants, I will review psychoanalytic findings about why individuals have prejudice and how societal prejudice evolves. This review is necessary for understanding why many persons in the host country, or even in the same country but in a different region, are sometimes afraid of newcomers, even the many who have suffered a great deal.

Scientific observations of infants during recent decades have taught us that an infant's mind is more active than we originally thought (see, for example, Bloom, 2010; Emde, 1991; Lehtonen, 2003; Stern, 1985). Studies on psychobiological potential for *we-ness* and bias toward our own kind are taking place. We are also observing how a sense of "we-ness" is passed to toddlers in the very early mother–child relationship. For example, researchers have found significant relations between aspects of Native American toddler socioemotional development and maternal reports of stress, and drug and/or alcohol use, but also, inter-estingly, Native American identity (Frankel, Croy, Kubicek, Emde, Mitchell & Spicer, 2014). Because the environment of the infant and very small child is restricted to parents, siblings, relatives, and other caregivers, the extent of "we-ness" does not include a distinct intellec-tual and emotional dimension of ethnicity, nationality, or other types of large-group identity. In the introductory chapter I stated that, as far as tribal affiliation, nationality, ethnicity, religion, or political ideology are concerned, infants and small children are *generalists* (Erikson, 1956). The subjective experience and deep intellectual knowledge of belonging to a large-group identity develops later in childhood.

I will begin by referring to the concept of "attachment," as we examine how an infant starts to know the Other and how "normal" prejudice develops. Psychoanalyst and well-known researcher of mother–child interactions Johannes Lehtonen has recently summarized neurophysiological and clinical findings on the development of a newborn infant's mind (Lehtonen, in press). He reminds us that after birth infants face an adaptation to brand new and radically different biological extra-uterine life. They need to initiate breathing and reflective sucking for gaining nutrients from their providers. Now, sensory stimuli, such as taste, smell, auditory signals, movements, and thumb sucking, will have vital implications for them. As Lehtonen states, clinical observations and research (Cheour et al., 2002; Denton, McKinley, Farrell & Egan, 2009; Hofer, 2014; Kandel, 2006; Lappi et al., 2007; Purhonen, Kilpeläinen-Lees, Valkonen-Korhonen, Karhu & Lehtonen, 2005) illustrate how the merger between infant and caretaker helps to build a soothing and life-supporting internal image in the infant to which sensations coming from inside the body contribute. The infant forms an attachment bond with the mother or the mothering adult (see also Fonagy & Target 1997; Winnicott, 1963). Through observing smiling and reciprocal vocalization of infants around the age of two to three months we note that they begin to develop internal images of external beings, even though at this time such images are not stabilized or fully differentiated from other such images. From a theoretical point of view, we can state that the preparation for the concept of the *Other* for an individual begins to emerge while the infant experiences attachment to mother and specific persons, a process that will take about three years to stabilize.

There is a well-known concept in psychoanalysis known as *stranger anxiety*: infants' recognition that not all the faces around them belong to their caregivers. At eight months of life, the baby fears the stranger/ Other who, in reality, has done nothing harmful to them. A normal phenomenon in human development, stranger anxiety is a response to the stranger/Other in the infant's mind and becomes the foundation for the evolution of future "normal" prejudice. We realize that the infant starts differentiating between stranger/Other and familiar/Other (Parens, 1979; Spitz, 1965).

The attachment to the familiar Other is necessary for the development of the infant's mind and adaptation to life. As they grow, infants begin to separate their own mental images from images of all types of others, and later integrate different aspects of both types of images (Kernberg, 1976; Mahler, 1968; Volkan, 1976). Theoretically speaking, identification can take place after children separate their self-representation from object images. Children identify with realistic, fantasized, wished-for, or even scary aspects of important individuals in their environment. They take in such individuals' mothering, fathering, sibling, and mentoring functions, and psychological ways of handling problems. What is taken in influences the children's own unconscious fantasies (Volkan, 2010) and their role in developing personality characteristics. Children's identifications with individuals who are close to them include their investments in concrete or abstract large-group identity markers, such as physical characteristics, language, nursery rhymes, food, dances, religious beliefs, myths, flags, geographical investments, heroes, martyrs, and images of historical events. These are utilized to expand their internal worlds in relating to their own small group and, when they grow older, to their large group as well. Freud (1940a) held that parents are the representatives of society for their children. Children also come to identify with parents' and other important persons' prejudicial attitudes. They slowly stop being "generalists."

Now let me focus on another concept described in Chapter Five: depositing. This can be seen as Melanie Klein's (1946) description of "projective identification," but by this term I describe the creation of a kind of "psychological DNA" within the child, an element of the foundation for identity formation. Judith Kestenberg's (1982) term "transgenerational transposition," Christopher Bollas' (1987) term "extractive introjections," Anne Ancelin Schützenberger's (1998) term "ancestor syndrome," and Haydée Faimberg's (2005) description of "the telescoping of generations" refer to depositing traumatized images. Judith Kestenberg's (1980) and Yolanda Gambel's (1983), as well as Ira Brenner's (2004, 2014) stories related to "Holocaust culture" also illustrate depositing. Within the psychoanalytic literature there are many other examples of how survivors of the Holocaust have passed images and tasks to their offspring and how these offspring psychologically responded to such transgenerational transmissions in ways ranging from creative to troublesome (for references, see Brenner, 2004, 2014; Volkan, Ast & Greer, 2002). For example, I studied the life of a man who as a child was a "reservoir" for the extremely traumatized image of his father figure, who was a survivor of the Bataan Death March and the Japanese prison camps in the Philippines. This child grew up to become a sadistic animal killer because the task deposited in him was to be a "hunter," instead of being the hunted one as his father figure had been (Volkan, 2014a). Through being reservoirs of deposited images and the tasks given to them in order to deal with these images, children's psychology becomes linked to the history of their families and often these families' ancestors' histories, especially the traumatic ones and various types of prejudice.

After experiencing a collective catastrophe inflicted by an enemy group, affected individuals are left with self-images similarly (though not identically) traumatized by the massive event. These many individuals deposit such images into their children and give them tasks, such as, "Regain my self-esteem for me," "Put my mourning process on the right track," "Be assertive and take revenge," or, "Never forget and remain alert." Though each child in the second generation owns an individualized identity, all share similar links to the same massive trauma's image and similar unconscious tasks for coping with it. If the next generation cannot effectively fulfill their shared tasks—and this is usually the case—they will pass them on to the third generation, and so on. Such conditions create a powerful unseen network among thousands, sometimes millions, of people. As decades pass, the mental image of the ancestors' historical event with references to heroes, martyrs, victimization, and other feelings continues to link all the individuals in the large group. For the new generations, the meaning of the tasks go through what psychoanalysts call *change of function* (Waelder, 1936); now the mental image of the event emerges as a most significant large-group identity marker, a "chosen trauma" (Volkan, 1991, 2006, 2013, 2014c). A large group does not "choose" to be victimized by another large group and subsequently lose self-esteem, but it does "choose" to psychologize and dwell on a past traumatic event and make it a major large-group identity marker.

Another concept related to the understanding of the Other is known in psychoanalysis as "individuation." As the child's mind develops she also, psychologically speaking, pushes mother, the familiar Other, and other caregivers away in an intrapsychic process, in order to "separate and individuate" (Mahler, 1968). Others—those who are close and important to us as family members, friends, and competitors—are at the unconscious level also parts of ourselves because of our identifications with them, because of our being reservoirs of what they have deposited into us to one degree or another, and because of our use of them as temporary or longer-term reservoirs of our own unwanted but sometimes wished-for images. By drawing close to such others and distancing from them, we continue to remain connected with actual life experiences, sexual and aggressive desires, conscious and unconscious fantasies, and individualized as well as shared prejudice. As the child grows up, the Other, both familiar and stranger, also becomes a concept beyond referring to the external mother or mothering person, a father, a sibling, another family member, a teacher, a friend, and people in the neighborhood across the park that the parents prohibited the child from passing through during his early years. The Other now has societal implications: it is a large group of beings who do not belong to the child's sense of "we-ness."

In this book, unless stated otherwise, such as when I refer to the "familiar Other," I use the term "Other" when it has societal implications. For a person and for those who share the same large-group sentiments with this person, the "Other" represents foreigners who have a different large-group identity. This term also applies to those, like Abkhazian Georgians, who belong to the some ethnic identity but have a different tribal affiliation and live at a different geographical location than those who treat them as newcomers.

Earlier I introduced "suitable targets of externalization," yet another concept that contributes to the evolution of large-group identity as well as the concept of the shared, large-group Other (Volkan, 1988, 2013, 2014c). When infants become children they begin to notice that certain things are special for their large groups, and some other things do not belong to their large group. Adults in children's environment provide them with shared targets, mostly inanimate objects, the utilization of which "teaches" children *experientially* what belongs to their large group and what does not. Children's investment in suitable targets of externalization is the true beginning of social/political investment in their own large group as well as prejudice against the Other—the large group's *need* to have allies and enemies (Volkan, 1988).

To illustrate what I am describing, let us turn to the island of Cyprus, where Greeks and Turks lived side by side for centuries until the island was *de facto* divided into two political entities in 1974. Greek farmers there often raise pigs. Turkish children, like Greek children, are invariably drawn to farm animals. Let us visualize that a four-year-old Cypriot Turkish child wants to touch and love a piglet. The mother or other important individuals in the Turkish child's environment would strongly discourage this. For Muslim Turks, the pig is "dirty." Cypriot Turkish farmers do not raise pigs; pigs exist only on Cypriot Greek farms. Accordingly, the pig does not belong to the Turks' large group and for the Turkish child the pig will be perceived as a cultural amplifier for the Greeks. Since Muslim Turks do not eat pork, in a concrete sense what is externalized into the image of the pig will not be re-internalized. Now the Turkish child has found a reservoir for externalizing *permanently* his "unwanted parts."

What do I mean by "unwanted parts"? Infants and small children have loving and frustrating experiences when relating to their mothers and other caregivers, including "good" feeding and "bad" feeding experiences (Stern, 1985). Small children need time to integrate their "loved" and "unloved" parts and correspondingly "loving" and "frustrating" images of the mother and other persons. Around the age of three, the child, for all practical purposes, achieves integration of libidinally and aggressively loaded self- and object images. The task of putting together "black" and "white" representations in order to make "gray" is not, however, an isolated process. Tensions pertaining to object relations conflict persist to some extent, and the child must find different ways dealing with them while engaged in the task of making grays. Some unintegrated "unwanted" aspects of the self and caretakers, as well as "wanted" ones, remain in the mind of the child. What happens to the unintegrated self and object images? They may find their way into the developing superego structure or they may be repressed (Kernberg, 1976; Van der Waals, 1952), or they may be externalized into suitable targets.

For Cypriot Turkish children, the pig is a suitable reservoir for their "unwanted" images. Unintegrated "wanted" images also find suitable targets of permanent externalization that, as the child grows, represent "we-ness" and become significant large-group identity markers. For example, Finnish children use the sauna and Scottish children use the wearing of kilts for their libidinalized "good" reservoirs.

Stable externalizations of both libidinally loaded and aggressively loaded unintegrated self- and object images can be achieved due to the existence of targets or reservoirs that are supported culturally, socially, and politically. These targets or reservoirs are initially inanimate and nonhuman objects, such as one's national colors for "good" images and the neighboring countries' national colors for "bad" images. John Mack (1979) spoke of these objects as "cultural amplifiers" that refer to those symbols that have similar meanings for all the adults as a specific large group. Children not only possess certain cultural amplifiers, such as language, nursery rhymes, food, dances, religious symbols, or specific geographical locations through identifications with important others in their environment, they also make these amplifiers "good" targets of permanent externalization. The Other's cultural amplifiers are available to become "bad" reservoirs.

When the small Turkish child experiences a piglet as a target of externalization, he does not fully understand what Greekness means. And only when Finnish children grow up will they have sophisticated thoughts and feelings about Finnishness. Sophisticated thoughts, perceptions associated with emotions, and historical images of the Other as a large group and about one's own large group evolve much later. People grow up without an awareness that the symbol of the Other was originally in the service of helping them as children to avoid feeling tensions due to keeping some unwanted parts within. When the child finds a suitable target for "unwanted parts," the precursor of the Other as a large group becomes established in the child's mind at an *experimental level*. While holding on to their own personal identities, tens, hundreds of thousands, or millions of children utilize the same suitable targets to externalize their unwanted or idealized parts, contributing to the evolution of large-group identities. I have theorized that suitable targets of externalization become building blocks for the subsequent structuring of ethnic, national, cultural, religious, and ideological large-group identities (Volkan, 1988).

Religious cults and terrorist organizations such as ISIS also show us that people can be attracted, in their *adulthood*, to becoming members of *a different type of large group*. Such large groups exist as long as they have a mission—religious, ideological, or terroristic—to carry out. If a person becomes a member of a large group like ISIS as an adult, the person perceives the existence of elements representing "good" suitable targets in that large group. The same person sees representations of "bad" suitable targets in the enemy of the new large group. The enemy evolves as dangerous, and its destruction may be perceived as the expected thing to do without guilt and moral considerations.

Psychological investment in suitable, shared reservoirs creates a basis for pre-oedipal relations at the large-group level. In the psychoanalytic literature, we find oedipal considerations in the establishment of large-group identities and in the interactions between large groups. For me, both considerations are correct. I contend that the foundation of the core large-group identity is created during the pre-oedipal period; oedipal influences, however important, are added later. Ernst Kris (1975) states that when there are "common symbols of identification" the psycho-logical ties between members of a large group are established (p. 468). He goes on to state that large-group cohesion can be strengthened by "a common ideal or tradition or by admiration for a common leader—in brief, by unity in devotion" (p. 469), and that one of the strongest, if not *the* strongest, motives is power, for maintaining the integrity of a large group. Its social distance from other large groups is "the fear of competition" (p. 468), such as economic competition. According to Kris, economic hardship causes an increase in prejudice.

One catches the reflection of oedipal elements we see in individuals—competition with and submission to an oedipal father—in Kris' focus on large-group barriers and large-group prejudice. Other psychoana-lysts have also considered oedipal factors in the establishment of large-group identity. For example, Chasseguet-Smirgel (1984) refers to the successful resolution of the Oedipus complex as the factor influencing the child's entrance into the father's universe. Narendra Keval (2016) came to Britain in the 1970s and observed racist graffiti on the walls of houses in the neighborhood where he lived. This was, I believe, one key motivation for him to write a book on how voluntary and forced emigration may create major headaches and heartbreaks. In his book he also presents racist scenes from South Africa. Theoretically speak-ing, he connects a racist scene with a primal scene: the child's fantasy of parent's lovemaking and being left out. He also connects the arrival of a black teenager in a playground of white teenagers to sibling rivalry issues. In summary, while each individual has an individual identity, she also shares with others in a large group certain identifications, deposited images, "good" suitable targets of externalizations, ways of handling oedipal competitions, and certain fantasies. All these make the evolution of "normal" prejudice part of the evolution of the human mind.

What I write about here also finds support from considerations about the historical evolution of the human race. Erik Erikson (1956) developed the idea that human beings have evolved, by whatever kind of evolution and for whatever adaptive reasons, into *pseudo species*, such as tribes or clans, which behave as if they are separate species. He theorized that primitive humans sought a measure of protection for their unbearable nakedness by adopting the armor of the lower animals and wearing their skins, feathers, or claws. On the basis of these outer garments, each tribe, clan, or group developed a sense of shared identity, as well as a conviction that it alone harbored *the one human identity*. I can also add another idea, also speculative, that may further explain what happened during the course of human evolution and how human large groups have been able to kill one another while feeling that each belongs to a different species. For centuries, neighboring tribes or clans had only each other to interact with, due to their natural boundaries. Neighboring groups had to compete for territory, food, sex, and physical goods for their survival. Eventually, this primitive level of competition assumed more psychological implications. Physical essentials, besides retaining their status as genuine necessities, absorbed mental meanings as well—such as narcissism, competition, prestige, honor, power, envy, revenge, humiliation, submission, grief, and mourning—and evolved from being tokens of survival to becoming large-group symbols, cultural amplifiers, traditions, religions, or historical memories that embedded a large group's self-esteem, narcissism, and identity.

Such postulations are supported by references to the Other in many ancient documents and languages. The ancient Chinese regarded themselves as *people* and viewed the Other as *kuei* or "hunting spirits." The Apache Indians considered themselves to be *indeh*, "the people," and everyone else as *indah*, "the enemy" (Boyer, 1986). The Munduruku in the Brazilian rainforest divided their world into Munduruku, who were people, and non-Munduruku, who were *pariwat* (enemies), except for certain neighbors who they perceived as friendly (Murphy, 1957). Anthropologist Howard Stein (1990) believes that this type of pattern cannot be literally generalized to all cultures, but it shows the communality about the sense of "otherness," and shared prejudices. In the recorded history available to us, we constantly see interactions between "pseudo species," with one group seeing the other as less than human in malignant ways. In the next chapter I will examine immigrants and refugees as the Other and also consider how the "normal" prejudice about them becomes hostile and even malignant.

CHAPTER TEN

Border psychology and fear of newcomers

This chapter will examine newcomers as the Other who passes through the border surrounding the host people. To illustrate the appearance and consequences of shared prejudice against displaced people and immigrants, especially when there is an influx of newcomers from a different cultural, religious, or linguistic background, I will return to my big tent metaphor (Volkan, 2003a) and examine border psychology.

Here we must think in terms of how individuals learn to wear two main layers, like fabric, from the time they stabilize their memberships in an ethnic or other type of large group during their childhood or from the time they join a cult, guerrilla, or terrorist group during their adulthood. The first layer, the individual layer, fits each of them snugly, like clothing. It is one's core personal identity, which provides an inner sense of persistent sameness for the individual (Erikson, 1956). The second layer is like the canvas of a big tent, which is loose fitting, but allows a huge number of individuals to share a sense of sameness with others under the same large-group tent. Threads that make up the canvas of the tent are primarily shared identifications and shared "good" targets of externalization. As Maurice Apprey (1993) illustrates in his writings on African American large-group identity, others'—in this case white Americans'—externalizations and projections can be absorbed into the fabric of the large-group tent's canvas. In order to understand this last idea, picture two large-group tents side by side. Individuals in the first tent throw mud, excrement, and refuse—that is, they externalize their "bad" images of themselves and others, and project their own unwanted thoughts, feelings, attitudes, and expectations—onto the canvas of the second tent. Note that this action is taken toward the large-group identity itself, the canvas, and not necessarily toward the individuals who possess this group identity. The stain left from the mud, excrement, and refuse is absorbed into the identity of the large group that receives it. The "bad" images, thoughts, and affects that are externalized, projected, or displaced by the neighboring large group can become a component of the receiver group's large-group identity. Apprey concludes that American white people's perceptions of black people have been assimilated into the African American large-group identity experience. He sees how black-on-black crime has become a modified version of the mental representation of white–black historical interactions. Other designs reflect many types of cultural, religious, and historical amplifiers (Mack, 1979).

Each large group's tent canvas is decorated with special designs symbolizing the large group's cultural and religious "amplifiers," among them, those representing images of ancestors' historical realistic or fantasized events: chosen traumas and chosen glories. In the last chapter I described chosen traumas. All large groups also have ritualistic recollections of events and heroes whose mental representations include a shared feeling of success and triumph among group members. Such events and persons appearing in these recollections are heavily mythologized over time, and the mental representations become large-group markers, which I call "chosen glories." Chosen glories are passed on to succeeding generations through transgenerational transmissions made in parent–child or teacher–child interactions and through participation in ceremonies recalling past successful events. Sometimes designs for chosen glories appear mixed with designs of chosen traumas on the tent canvas. New historical events combined with the influences of "charismatic" (Abse & Ulman, 1977; Volkan, 2004; Weber, 1923) or "transforming" (Burns, 1978) leaders, such as Lenin, Atatürk, Gandhi, and Mao, can change such designs on the tent canvas. Such leaders bring hundreds of thousands or millions of people out of political isolation and into a new kind of political participation. Sometimes these leaders go a step further: driven to meet the requirements of their own internal worlds, they reshape the external world of their followers and their subjective feelings about their large-group identity.

In our world today we are constantly exposed to terroristic activities. This type of large group also provides a metaphorical huge tent for people seeking a place where they can find a cause and thus support their self-esteem. The main design used for this type of large-group tent canvas includes images of chosen trauma, reflecting past victimizations that allow the group members to feel entitled to perform horrifying, immoral acts to reverse their sense of victimization and create an image of glory, even though this glory, in their illusion, is expected to come about just before the apocalypse (Suistola & Volkan, in press). When individuals, such as suicide bombers, consider this secondary garment as their primary layer of clothing, they are under the influence of large-group psychology.

Under a huge large-group tent there are subgroups and subgroup identities, such as professional and political identities. While it is the tent pole—the political leader and the governing body—that holds the tent erect, the tent's canvas psychologically protects the leader, other persons with authority, and all members of the large group (Volkan & Fowler, 2009a). Dissenters in a large group do not change the essential shared sentiments within the large group unless, as in the case of terrorist organizations, they develop a huge number of followers who become an important subgroup and even a new, different type of large group, such as ISIS. From the viewpoint of individual psychology, a person may perceive the pole as a father figure (Freud, 1921c) and the canvas as a nurturing mother (Anzieu, 1984; Chasseguet-Smirgel, 1984; Kernberg 1980). From a large-group psychology point of view, the canvas represents the *psychological border* of large-group identity that is shared by tens, hundreds of thousands, or millions of people.

The existence of a psychological border has been acknowledged by politicians. For an explicit example of this, we can refer to then Egyptian president Anwar el-Sadat's historic 1977 visit to Israel when, before the Israeli parliament, he expressed a desire to move beyond political concerns to a more profound reconciliation. He referred to a psychological "wall" between his country and Israel:

> Yet there remains another wall. This wall constitutes a psychological barrier between us, a barrier of suspicion, a barrier of hallucination

without any action, deed, or decision, a barrier of distorted and eroded interpretation of every event and statement. It is this psychological barrier which I described in official statements as constituting 70 percent of the whole problem.

My work in international relations started after Sadat's visit to Jerusalem (Volkan, 2013, 2014b). When I participated in unofficial diplomatic meetings between representatives of Israel and Egypt, I could then begin to examine the concept of the "psychological border" closely. Such an examination gained more support when I was involved in bringing together, again unofficially, representatives of other large groups in conflict. At such times, the rituals between the representatives of opposing groups mainly center on attempts at repairing, protecting, and maintaining their large-group identities. For example, a ritual that I named the "accordion phenomenon" frequently occurs. After some airing of each group's past glories and listing of historical grievances, which themselves are carried out ritualistically, the opposing representatives become "friendly." This closeness, however, is followed by a sudden withdrawal from one another and then again by closeness. The pattern repeats numerous times. I liken this to the playing of an accordion—squeezing together and then pulling apart.

During the Arab–Israeli unofficial dialogue series, for example, there would be sudden unity among the opposing participants, during which the antagonists would enthusiastically note their mutual similarities. Statements such as, "We are all brothers and sisters, descendants of a common grandfather, Abraham!" would be heard during these periods of unity. But before long, participants from opposing groups would reassert their difference and distance from one another, and the cycle of contradictory attitudes would continue.

Derivatives of the aggression largely account for the accordion phenomenon; each party brings to such meetings its historical injuries and conflicts, chosen traumas and chosen glories, and experiences both conscious and unconscious feelings of aggression toward the "enemy." Initial distancing is thus a defensive maneuver to keep aggressive attitudes and feelings in check, since a meeting between opponents carries the potential for fantasized, symbolic, or real violence and corresponding retaliation. The existence of shared prejudice in the mind of large-group representatives is "normal." Enemies are real when they are shooting and killing us; they are also fantasized because they are reservoirs of our unwanted externalizations and projections. When opposing teams are confined in one room, sharing intense conscious efforts for peace, they must deny their aggressive and prejudicial feeling. This becomes oppressive when the closeness is perceived as a threat to each teams' identity. Blurring of one's own group identity is consciously and unconsciously perceived as dangerous, and so distancing occurs again.

At an official diplomatic negotiating table, such psychopolitical preoccupations are hidden behind high-level, calculated arguments, bargaining, and strategies (secondary-process activities). When threats to large-group identity are perceived, however, the psychological need to protect the large-group identity through rituals is exaggerated. This, in turn, may intrude into "rational" thinking and result in distortion or resistance to change and peace. When conducting unofficial diplomatic dialogues between enemy representatives, we paid attention to maintaining a psychological border between the opposing delegates, thus maintaining "non-sameness." In this way, representatives of opposing groups can be made to feel more comfortable and are ready to have more realistic political discussions and make decisions and come to agreements (Volkan, 1997, 1999, 2013).

As my experience in international relations expanded, I noted how physical borders can also become psychological borders. In 1986 I witnessed Anwar Sadat's description of a psychological wall between Israelis and Arabs. When tensions between Israelis and Jordanians were running hot, I visited the Allenby Bridge over the Jordan River that separates the two countries. I noted that the commercial trucks that travelled over the bridge looked as though the factory had forgotten to finish them; doors and hoods were missing, and even the upholstery had been removed so that contraband could be detected more easily. Although the same trucks crossed the border each day, Israeli customs officers would spend hours taking them apart and putting them back together to assure that nothing was smuggled in from Jordan. The Israelis would also routinely sweep a dirt road that ran parallel to the border, in order to detect the footprints of people attempting to cross it, even though the border was already protected by sophisticated electronic surveillance devices, mine fields, dozens of sentries, and hundreds of soldiers, not to mention the natural barrier of the Jordan River. Even if the extra precaution were justified, most likely the notion of a psychological border had intertwined itself with the physical border at this location. Such ritualistic activities, above and beyond being militarily realistic, were also employed to create a psychological separation between the two countries.

Defining and maintaining physical borders has always been vital to international and large-group relationships, but closer examination reveals that an effective psychological border is far more essential than simply a physical one. In fact, it may be said that a physical border succeeds only when it signifies a sufficient psychological one. Donald Winnicott (1969) noted that some political divisions, like the border between England and Wales, were based on mountains or other geographical features. But unlike such borders, which Winnicott believed to have a natural and meaningful beauty, he saw the man-made Berlin Wall as being ugly—an unnatural barrier born of international conflict. Nevertheless, Winnicott acknowledged a positive aspect of the Berlin Wall, suggesting that a dividing line between opposing forces, "at its worst postpones conflict and at its best holds opposing forces away from each other for long periods of time so that people may play and pursue the arts of peace" (p. 224). Such arts, he said, "belong to the temporary success of a dividing line between opposing forces; the lull between times when the wall has ceased to segregate good and bad" (p. 224).

When anxiety and regression take place within large groups in conflict, a simple line between them is not enough to protect the antagonists' identities. Any possibility of interpenetration has to be defended against, and under stressful and regressed conditions, physical borders assume high psychological significance. The border, perceived as a gap, clearly separates the two groups, a division that allows them to feel uncontaminated. This gap also stabilizes each large group's mutual projections and externalizations. Further, ritualization is used to define and strengthen the separation of large-group identities.

Reliance on the maintenance of non-sameness and a psychological border becomes more pronounced when stress and anxiety increase. At such times, an assortment of rituals for maintaining the two principles gain in prominence: exaggerating major differences, elevating minor differences to significant proportions, utilizing more shared symbols to patch up large-group identities, reactivating historical grievances and glories. The members of the large group experience physical borders as psychological skins.

All people have probably experienced some aspect of the psychological importance of borders, whether through customs and immigration controls; geographic borders, such as mountains and rivers, that separate nations or other territories; or the fences and walls that separate neighboring individuals. This principle was observable for me when I had opportunities to look closely at exaggerated physical borders between enemies beside Allenby Bridge, including the Green Line in Cyprus and the former Berlin Wall. Along such borders, elaborate rituals are common, including ceremonial changing of guards, constant monitoring and maintenance, and complex protocols and practices.

Shared prejudices are utilized in the service of maintaining and protecting large-group identity, which in turn also helps to maintain and protect individual identity. Groups, small and large, are made up of people. What we observe in individual psychology is reflected in small- or large-group psychology. But once prejudice is shared, it develops its own life, its own storyline that is related to shared identity. Over three decades, Michael Diamond and Seth Allcorn (2009) from the Harry S. Truman School of Public Affairs, University of Missouri have carried out psychoanalytically informed field work for organizational improvement. They describe regressed organizations that may become divided into what they call "silos," which are identity units with certain shared affects attached to them. For example, an organization's branch in the north of a city affectively separates itself from southern and western units, and all branches begin to relate to one another in a prejudicial manner.

We can imagine the unprecedented surge of migrants and refugees currently flooding into Europe as representing the Other which is threatening the stability of host countries' psychological borders. Many individuals in these countries are terrified that their countries' social customs and economies will be damaged, that they will not be able to support the massive influx of newcomers. Psychologically speaking, the main fear is the contamination of their large-group identity by the identity of the Other. Those who are able to keep their individual identities from the impact of large-group sentiments become more willing to open the tent's door and accept the huge number of newcomers. Those who perceive the newcomers as tearing holes in, and thus damaging, the metaphorical large-group tent's canvas—the border of large-group identity—become anxious and defensively perceive the huge immigrant population as a major threat. When there is an event such as the Paris, San Bernardino, and Brussels attacks, their xenophobia becomes more generalized. They may develop hostile, even malignant, shared prejudice. The polarization in the host country leads to new political and social concerns and complications. Some politicians and others focus on not only major differences, but also minor differences (Volkan, 1988, 1997, 2004) between the newcomers and the people in the host country, increasing attention to large-group identity issues in order to gain votes or popularity. The population in the host country becomes contaminated with the impact of large-group psychology, and maintaining large-group identity becomes, consciously, but also unconsciously, the shared primary aim. When this impact increases, the shared prejudice can no longer stay benign. At such times focus is on psychological borders. Throughout history physical borders have been built not only to protect the physical existence of a large group of persons, but also their psychological "purity," to protect from contamination by the Other. For example, the Iron Curtain was not only a physical border, but also a psychological one. As I write this book, the idea of the "beautiful wall," proposed by Donald Trump for our borders, is also attracting attention, because the idea behind it responds to large-group psychology.

Focusing on psychological aspects of a refugee crisis should not interfere with our understanding and evaluation of realistic and practical issues, as well as security concerns, even though many of them become contaminated with emotional attitudes. Obviously, credible realistic and practical issues and security concerns need to be dealt with in the best way possible by authorities and organizations assigned to handle them. As I have been writing this book I have watched on television the present-day refugees in Europe and elsewhere. In the conditions they currently endure, a psychoanalyst cannot carry out psychoanalytic treatment of such individuals, but training in psychoanalytic theory and experience in intensive clinical work provide psychoanalysts with some tools to understand and help refugees in unique ways. Psychoanalysts can become consultants and trainers to local mental health professionals, helping them notice and understand issues—such as what it meant when Abkhazia refugee Dali did not want to apply for a new identity card, or the role of Charlie the dog—and they can help seek out "entry points," such as looking for settlement "leaders" and working with them. Also, I find it extremely important and necessary to write papers and books, and give talks about the psychology of newcomers and hosts, in order to bring such knowledge to the public's attention. We need to find out if such activities might tame shared anxiety as well as hostile prejudice. People exposed to fantasized psychological dangers may, through access to a wider perspective, gain a better way of dealing with realistic problems and actual dangers. This may be wishful thinking on my part, but nevertheless, my long experience in international relations urges me to make the above statement. With a focus on large-group psychology in its own right, and especially by describing elements specific to large-group identities and the rituals carried out to protect them, the door has opened for a dialogue between psychoanalysts and specialists in international relations, including educators, those in charge of refugee issues, and perhaps even some politicians. There is beauty in human diversity, and most people can enjoy human diversity when they are not preoccupied with the pressures and anxieties associated with the maintenance of their large-group tent's canvas. Recognizing this beauty, however, often requires a great deal of work, and I believe that psychoanalysts, when they are willing to become involved in interdisciplinary efforts, have much to offer those who wish to encourage diversity while resolving incredibly difficult realistic problems.

REFERENCES

Abse, D. W., & Ulman, R. B. (1977). Charismatic political leadership and collective regression. In: R. S. Robons (Ed.), *Psychopathology and Political Leadership* (pp. 35–52). New Orleans, LA: Tulane University Press.

Akhtar, S. (1999a). Age at migration: An introductory overview. *Mind and Human Interaction*, 10: 3–10.

Akhtar, S. (1999b). *Immigration and Identity: Turmoil, Treatment and Transformation*. Northvale, NJ: Jason Aronson.

Akhtar, S. (2009). *Comprehensive Dictionary of Psychoanalysis*. London: Karnac.

Anzieu, D. (1984). *The Group and the Unconscious*. London: Routledge & Kegan Paul.

Apprey, M. (1993). The African-American experience: Forced immigration and transgenerational trauma. *Mind and Human Interaction*, 4: 70–75.

Ast, G. (1991). Interviews with Germans about reunification. *Mind and Human Interaction*, 2: 100–104.

Bloom, P. (2010). *How Pleasure Works: The New Science of Why We Like What We Like*. New York: W. W. Norton.

Blos, P. (1968). Character formation in adolescence. *Psychoanalytic Study of the Child*, 23: 245–263.

Blos, P. (1979). *The Adolescent Passage: Developmental Issues*. New York: International Universities Press.

105

Bollas, C. (1987). *The Shadow of the Object: Psychoanalysis of the Unthought Known*. London: Free Association.

Bonovitz, J., & Ergas, R. (1999). The affective experience of the child immigrant: Issues of loss and mourning. *Mind and Human Interaction*, 10: 15–25.

Bowlby, J., & Parkes, C. M. (1970). Separation and loss within the family. In: E. J. Anthony & C. Koupernick (Eds), *The Child in His Family*, Vol. 1 (pp. 197–216). New York: Wiley Interscience.

Boyer, L. B. (1983). *The Regressed Patient*. New York: Jason Aronson.

Boyer, L. B. (1986). One man's need to have enemies: A psychoanalytic perspective. *Journal of Psychoanalytic Anthropology*, 9: 101–120.

Boyer, L. B. (1999). *Countertransference and Regression*. Northvale, NJ: Jason Aronson.

Brenner, I. (2004). *Psychic Trauma: Dynamics, Symptoms, and Treatment*: Lanham, MD: Jason Aronson.

Brenner, I. (2014). *Dark Matters: Exploring the Realm of Psychic Devastation*. London: Karnac.

Burns, J. M. (1978). *Leadership*. New York: Harper Torchbooks.

Bychowski, G. (1952). *Psychotherapy of Psychosis*. New York: Grune & Stratton.

Chasseguet-Smirgel, J. (1984). *The Ego Ideal*. New York: W. W. Norton.

Cheour, M., Martynova, O., Näätänen, R., Erkkola, R., Sillanpää, M., Kero, P., Raz, A., Kaipio, M. L., Hiltunen, J., Aaltonen, O., Savela, J., & Hämäläinen, H. (2002). Speech sounds learned by sleeping newborns. *Nature, 415*: 599–600.

Copelman, D. (1993). The immigrant Experience: Margin notes. *Mind and Human Interaction*, 4: 76–82.

Denton, D. A., McKinley, M. J., Farrell, M., & Egan G. F. (2009). The role of primordial emotions in the evolutionary origin of consciousness. *Consciousness and Cognition, 18*: 500–514.

Diamond, M., & Allcorn, S. (2009). *Private Selves in Public Organizations: The Psychodynamics of Organizational Diagnosis and Change*. New York: Palgrave.

Dietrich, D. R. (1989). Early childhood parent death, psychic trauma and organization, and object death. In: D. R. Dietrich & P. C. Shabad (Eds), *Problem of Loss and Mourning: Psychoanalytic Perspectives* (pp. 277–335). Madison, CT: International Universities Press.

Elovitz, P., & Kahn, C. (1997). *Immigrant Experiences: Personal Narrative and Psychological Analysis*. Cranbury, NJ: Associated University Press.

Emde, R. N. (1991). Positive emotions for psychoanalytic theory: Surprises from infancy research and new directions. *Journal of the American Psychoanalytic Association, 39* (Supplement): 5–44.

Erikson, E. H. (1956). The problem of ego identity. *Journal of the American Psychoanalytic Association, 4*: 56–121.

Erikson, E. H. (1963). *Childhood and Society*. New York: W. W. Norton.

Faimberg, H. (2005). *The Telescoping of Generations: Listening to the Narcissistic Links Between Generations*. London: Routledge.

Fintzy, R. T. (1971). Vicissitudes of the transitional object in a borderline child. *International Journal of Psychoanalysis, 52*: 107–114.

Fonagy, P., & Target, M. (1997). Attachment and reflective function: Their role in self-organization. *Development and Psychopathology, 9*: 679–700.

Frankel, K. A., Croy, C. D., Kubicek, L. F., Emde, R. N., Mitchell, C. M., & Spicer, P. (2014). Toddler socioemotional behavior in a northern Plains Indian tribe: Associations with maternal psychosocial well-being. *Infant Mental Health Journal, 35*: 10–20.

Frej, W. (2015). Venezuela plans to take in 20,000 Syrian refugees. *The World Post, 8 September*. Available at: www.huffingtonpost.com/entry/venezuela-maduro-syrian-refugees_us_55cf279cc4b03784e276bc8b

Freud, A. (1958). Adolescence. *Psychoanalytic Study of the Child, 13*: 255–278.

Freud, S. (1917e). Mourning and melancholia. *S.E., 14*: 237–258. London: Hogarth.

Freud, S. (1920g). *Beyond the Pleasure Principle*. *S.E., 18*: 7–64. London: Hogarth.

Freud, S. (1921c). *Group Psychology and the Analysis of the Ego*. *S.E., 18*: 67–143. London: Hogarth.

Freud, S. (1940a). *An Outline of Psycho-analysis*. *S.E., 23*: 211–253. London: Hogarth.

Freud, S. (1940e). Splitting of the ego in the process of defence. *S.E., 23*: 271–278. London: Hogarth.

Furman, E. (1974). *A Child's Parent Dies: Studies in Childhood Bereavement*. New Haven, CT: Yale University Press.

Furman, R. (1973). A child's capacity for mourning. In: E. J. Anthony & C. Koupernick (Eds), *The Child in His Family: The Impact of Disease and Death*, Vol. 2 (pp. 225–231). New York: John Wiley.

Garza-Guerrero, A. C. (1974). Culture shock: Its mourning and vicissitudes of identity. *Journal of the American Psychoanalytic Association, 22*: 400–429.

Greenacre, P. (1970). The transitional object and the fetish: With special reference to the role of illusion. *International Journal of Psychoanalysis, 51*: 447–456.

Grinberg, L. (1992). *Guilt and Depression* (Trans. C. Trollope). London: Karnac.

Grinberg, L. & Grinberg, R. (1989). *Psychoanalytic Perspectives on Migration and Exile* (Trans. N. Festinger). New Haven, CT: Yale University Press.

Hartman, H. (1939). *Ego Psychology and Problems of Adaptation*. New York: International Universities Press, 1958.

Hofer, M. (2014). The emerging synthesis of development and evolution: A new biology for psychoanalysis. *Neuropsychoanalysis, 16*: 3–22.

Itzkowitz, N. (2001). Unity out of diversity. *Mind and Human Interaction, 12*: 173–175.

Jacobson, E. (1964). *The Self and the Object World.* New York: International Universities Press.

Jensen, L., Arnett, J. J., & McKenzie, J. (2011). Globalization and cultural identity. In: S. J. Schwartz, K. Luyckx, & V. L. Vignoles (Eds), *Handbook of Identity: Theory and Research* (pp. 285–301). New York: Springer Science.

Julius, D. A. (1992). Biculturalism and international interdependence. *Mind and Human Interaction, 3*: 53–56.

Kahn, C. (2008). *Undeterred, I Made It In America.* Bloomington, IN: AuthorHouse.

Kandel, E. R. (2006). *In Search of Memory: The Emergence of a New Science of Mind.* New York: W. W. Norton.

Kernberg, O. F. (1976). *Object Relations Theory and Clinical Psychoanalysis.* New York: Jason Aronson.

Kernberg, O. F. (1980). *Internal World and External Reality: Object Relations Theory Applied.* New York: Jason Aronson.

Kernberg, O. F. (1989). Mass psychology through the analytic lens. Paper presented at "Through the Looking Glass: Freud's Impact on Contemporary Culture." American College of Psychoanalysts Annual Meeting, Philadelphia, PA, 23 September.

Kernberg, O. F. (2010). Some observations on the process of mourning. *International Journal of Psychoanalysis, 91*: 601–619.

Kestenberg, J. S. (1980). Psychoanalyses of children of survivors from the Holocaust: Case presentations and assessment. *Journal of the American Psychiatric Association, 28*: 775–804.

Kestenberg, J. S. (1982). A psychological assessment based on analysis of a survivor's child. In: M. S. Bergman & M. E. Jucovy (Eds), *Generations of the Holocaust* (pp. 158–177). New York: Columbia University Press.

Keval, N. (2016). *Racist States of Mind: Understanding the Perversion of Curiosity and Concern.* London: Karnac.

Khundadze, N. (2000). *Sonnets with Pain* [translated from the original Georgian for this edition by Manana Gabashvili]. Tbilisi: Molodini.

Klein, M. (1940). Mourning and its relations to manic-depressive states. In: *Contributions to Psychoanalysis: 1921–1945* (pp. 311–338). London: Hogarth.

Klein, M. (1946). Notes on some schizoid mechanism. In: J. Riviere (Ed.), *Development in Psychoanalysis* (pp. 292–320). London: Hogarth.

Klein, M. (1950). *Narrative of a Child Analysis.* New York: Basic.

Kris, E. (1975). *Selected Papers of Ernst Kris.* New Haven, CT: Yale University Press.

Laplanche, J., & Pontalis, J. B. (1967). *The Language of Psycho-analysis* (Trans. D. N. Smith). New York: Norton.

Lappi, H., Valkonen-Korhonen, M., Georgiadis, S., Tarvainen, M. P., Tarkka, I. M., Karjalainen, P. A., & Lehtonen, J. (2007). Effects of nutritive and non-nutritive sucking on infant heart rate variability during the first 6 months of life. *Infant Behavior Development, 30*: 546–556.

Lehtonen, J. (2003). The dream between neuroscience and psychoanalysis: Has feeding an infant impact on brain function and the capacity to create dream images in infants? *Psychoanalysis in Europe, 57*: 175–182.

Lehtonen, J. (in press). The matrix of mind: The networks of the brain, and the principle of transformation in art therapy for psychosis. In: K. Killick (Ed.), *Art Therapy for Psychosis*. London: Routledge.

Lindemann, E. (1944). Symptomatology and management of acute grief. *American Journal of Psychiatry, 101*: 141–148.

Loewenberg, P. (1991). Uses of anxiety. *Partisan Review, 3*: 514–525.

Lorand, S. (1957). Book review: *New Directions in Psycho-analysis*, eds. M. Klein, et al. *International Journal of Psychoanalysis, 38*: 283–285.

Mack, J. E. (1979). Foreword. In: V. D. Volkan, *Cyprus: War and Adaptation* (pp. ix–xxi). Charlottesville, VA: University of Virginia Press.

Mahler, M. S. (1968). *On Human Symbiosis and the Vicissitudes of Individuation*. New York: International Universities Press.

Mahler, M. S., Pine, F., & Bergman, A. (1975). *The Psychological Birth of the Human Infant*. New York: Basic.

Meunier, S. (2000). The French exception. *Foreign Affairs, 79*: 104–116.

Mohamad, M. (2012). *The Malay Dilemma*. Singapore: Marshall Cavendish.

Moses, R., & Cohen, Y. (1993). An Israeli view. In: R. Moses (Ed.), *Persistent Shadows of the Holocaust: The Meaning to Those Not Directly Affected* (pp. 119–153). Madison, CT: International Universities Press.

Muller-Paisner, V. (2005). *Broken Chain: Catholics Uncover the Holocaust's Hidden Legacy and Discover Their Jewish Roots*. Charlottesville, VA: Pitchstone.

Murphy, R. F. (1957). Ingroup hostility and social cohesion. *American Anthropologist, 59*: 1018–1035.

Neubauer, P. B. (1993). Playing: Technical Implications. In: J. Solnit, D. J. Cohen, & P. B. Neubauer (Eds), *The Many Meanings of Play: A Psychoanalytic Perspective* (pp. 44–53). New Haven, CT: Yale University Press.

Niederland, W. G. (1961). The problem of the survivor. *Journal of the Hillside Hospital, 10*: 233–247.

Niederland, W. G. (1968). Clinical observations on the "survivor syndrome." *International Journal of Psychoanalysis, 49*: 313–315.

Ornstein, A., & Goldman, S. (2004). *My Mother's Eyes: Holocaust Memories of a Young Girl*. Covington, KY: Clerisy Press.

Ornstein, P., & Epstein, H. (2015). *Looking Back: Memoirs of a Psychoanalyst*. Lexington, MA: Plunkett Lake.

Parens, H. (1979). *The Development of Aggression in Early Childhood.* New York: Jason Aronson.

Parens, H. (2004). *Renewal of Life: Healing from the Holocaust.* Rockville, MD: Schreiber.

Pollock, G. H. (1961). Mourning and adaptation. *International Journal of Psychoanalysis, 42*: 341–361.

Pollock, G. H. (1989). *The Mourning–Liberation Process.* Vols 1 and 2. Madison, CT: International Universities Press.

Purhonen, M., Kilpeläinen-Lees, R., Valkonen-Korhonen, M., Karhu, J., & Lehtonen, J. (2005). Four-month-old infants process own mother's voice faster than unfamiliar voices—electrical signs of sensitization in infant brain. *Cognitive Brain Research, 3*: 627–633.

Rangell, L. (2003). Affects: In an individual and a nation. First Annual Volkan Lecture, 15 November, University of Virginia, Charlottesville, VA.

Rogers, R. (2000). Between Europe and America: Remembering and forgetting. *Mind and Human Interaction, 11*: 283–287.

Schützenberger, A. A. (1998). *The Ancestor Syndrome: Transgenerational Psychotherapy and the Hidden Links in the Family Tree.* New York: Routledge.

Searles, H. (1960). *The Nonhuman Environment in Normal Development and Schizophrenia.* New York: International Universities Press.

Šebek, M. (1992). Anality in the totalitarian system and the psychology of post-totalitarian society. *Mind and Human Interaction, 4*: 52–59.

Spitz, R. (1965). *The First Year of Life.* New York: International Universities Press.

Stein, H. F. (1980). *An Ethno-historic Study of Slovak-American Identity.* New York: Arno.

Stein, H. F. (1990). The international and group milieu of ethnicity: Identifying generic group dynamic issues. *Canadian Review of Studies in Nationalism, 17*: 107–130.

Stein, H. F. (1993). The Slovak- and Rusyn-American experience: Ethnic adaptation in the Steel Valley of Western Pennsylvania. *Mind and Human Interaction, 4*: 83–91.

Stern, D. N. (1985). *The Interpersonal World of the Infant: A View from Psychoanalysis and Developmental Psychology.* New York: Basic.

Streeck-Fischer, A. (2015). Identity formation difficulties in immigrant adolescents: Three cases from Germany. *American Journal of Psychoanalysis, 75*: 438–453.

Suistola, J., & Volkan, V. D. (in press, forthcoming 2017). *Gods Do Not Negotiate: Religious Knives and International Terror.* Durham, NC: Pitchstone.

Sullivan, H. S. (1962). *Schizophrenia as a Human Process.* New York: Norton.

Tähkä, V. (1984). Dealing with object loss. *Scandinavian Psychoanalytic Review, 7*: 13–33.

Tähkä, V. (1993). *Mind and its Treatment: A Psychoanalytic Approach*. Madison, CT: International Universities Press.

The Economist (2015). The home-grown threat, *417* (12 December 2015): p. 29.

Thomson, J. A., Harris, M., Volkan, V. D., & Edwards, B. (1995). The psychology of Western European neo-racism. *International Journal of Group Rights, 3*: 1–30.

Ticho, G. (1971). Cultural aspects of transference and countertransference. *Bulletin of the Menninger Clinic, 35*: 313–334.

Van der Waals, H. G. (1952). Discussion of the mutual influences in the development of ego and id. *Psychoanalytic Study of the Child, 7*: 66–68.

Van Essen, J. (1999). The capacity to live alone: Unaccompanied refugee minors in the Netherlands. *Mind and Human Interaction, 10*: 26–34.

Volkan, V. D. (1972). The "linking objects" of pathological mourners. *Archives of General Psychiatry, 27*: 215–222.

Volkan, V. D. (1976). *Primitive Internalized Object Relations: A Clinical Study of Schizophrenic, Borderline and Narcissistic Patients*. New York: International Universities Press.

Volkan, V. D. (1979). *Cyprus—War and Adaptation: A Psychoanalytic History of Two Ethnic Groups in Conflict*. Charlottesville, VA: University Press of Virginia.

Volkan, V. D. (1981). *Linking Objects and Linking Phenomena: A Study of the Forms, Symptoms, Metapsychology, and Therapy of Complicated Mourning*. New York: International Universities Press.

Volkan, V. D. (1988). *The Need to Have Enemies and Allies: From Clinical Practice to International Relationships*. Northvale, NJ: Jason Aronson.

Volkan, V. D. (1990a). Living statues and political decision making. *Mind and Human Interaction, 2*: 3–4, 19–20.

Volkan, V. D. (1990b). The question of Germany: A West German's response. *Mind and Human Interaction, 1*: 2–3, 9.

Volkan, V. D. (1991). On "chosen trauma." *Mind and Human Interaction, 3*: 13.

Volkan, V. D. (1995). *The Infantile Psychotic Self and its Fates: Understanding and Treating Schizophrenics and Other Difficult Patients*. Northvale, NJ: Jason Aronson.

Volkan, V. D. (1997). *Bloodlines: From Ethnic Pride to Ethnic Terrorism*. New York: Farrar, Straus & Giroux.

Volkan, V. D. (1999). Nostalgia as a linking phenomenon. *Journal of Applied Psychoanalytic Studies, 1*: 169–179.

Volkan, V. D. (2002). Foreword. In: K. Bell, A. Holder, P. Janssen, & J. van de Sande (Eds), *Migration and Persecution: Psychoanalytic Perspectives* (pp. 15–39). Giessen, Germany: Psychosozial-Verlag.

Volkan, V. D. (2003a). Large-group identity: Border psychology and related societal processes. *Mind and Human Interaction, 13*: 49–76.

Volkan, V. D. (2003b). The re-libidinalization of the internal world of a refugee family. *Group Analysis, 36*: 555–570.

Volkan, V. D. (2004). *Blind Trust: Large Groups and Their Leaders in Times of Crisis and Terror*. Charlottesville, VA: Pitchstone.

Volkan, V. D. (2006). *Killing in the Name of Identity: A Study of Bloody Conflicts*. Charlottesville, VA: Pitchstone.

Volkan, V. D. (2010). *Psychoanalytic Technique Expanded: A Textbook of Psychoanalytic Treatment*. Istanbul: OA Press.

Volkan, V. D. (2013). *Enemies on the Couch: A Psychopolitical Journey through War and Peace*. Durham, NC: Pitchstone.

Volkan, V. D. (2014a). *Animal Killer: Transmission of War Trauma from One Generation to the Next*. London: Karnac.

Volkan, V. D. (2014b). Father quest and linking objects: A story of the American World War II Orphans Network (AWON) and Palestinian orphans. In: P. Cohen, M. Sossin, & R. Ruth (Eds), *Healing in the Wake of Parental Loss: Clinical Applications and Therapeutic Strategies* (pp. 283–300). New York: Jason Aronson.

Volkan, V. D. (2014c). *Psychoanalysis, International Relations, and Diplomacy: A Sourcebook on Large-group Psychology*. London: Karnac.

Volkan, V. D. (2015). *A Nazi Legacy: A Study of Depositing, Transgenerational Transmission, Dissociation and Remembering Through Action*. London: Karnac.

Volkan, V. D., & Fowler, J. C. (2009a). Large-group narcissism and political leaders with narcissistic personality organization. *Psychiatric Annals, 39*: 214–222.

Volkan, V. D., & Fowler, J. C. (2009b). *Searching for a Perfect Woman: The Story of a Complete Psychoanalysis*. New York: Jason Aronson.

Volkan, V. D., & Itzkowitz, N. (1984). *The Immortal Atatürk: A Psychobiography*. Chicago, IL: University of Chicago Press.

Volkan, V. D., & Josephthal, D. (1980). The treatment of established pathological mourners. In: T. B. Karasu & L. Bellak (Eds). *Specialized Techniques in Individual Psychotherapy* (pp. 118–142). New York: Brunner/Mazel.

Volkan, V. D., & Zintl, E. (1993). *Life After Loss: Lessons of Grief*. New York: Charles Scribner's Sons.

Volkan, V. D., Ast, G., & Greer, W. F. (2002). *The Third Reich in the Unconscious: Transgenerational Transmission and its Consequences*. New York: Brunner-Routledge.

Volkan. V. D., Cilluffo, A. F., & Sarvay, T. L. (1975). Re-grief therapy and the function of the linking object as a key to stimulate emotionality. In: P. Olsen (Ed.), *Emotional Flooding* (pp. 179–224). New York: Behavioral.

Waelder, R. (1936). The principle of multiple function: Observations on multiple determination. *Psychoanalytic Quarterly, 5*: 45–62.

Wangh, M. (1992). Being a refugee and being an immigrant. *International Psychoanalysis, winter issue*: 15–17.

Weber, M. (1923). *Wirtschaft und Geselschaft [Economy and Society].* Vols 1 and 2. Tübingen, Germany: J.C.B. Mohr.

Werman, D. S. (1977). Normal and pathological nostalgia. *Journal of the American Psychoanalytic Association, 25*: 387–398.

Werman, D. S. (1984). The premature transference. Paper presented at the American Psychoanalytic Association Meeting, San Diego, California, 16–20 May.

Wilson, J. P., & Droždet, B. (2004). *Broken Spirits: The Treatment of Traumatized Asylum Seekers, Refugees, War and Torture Victims.* New York: Brunner-Routledge.

Winnnicott, D. W. (1953). Transitional objects and transitional phenomena: A study of the first not-me possession. *International Journal of Psycho-analysis, 34*: 89–97.

Winnicott, D. W. (1963). The value of depression. In: C. Winnicott, R. Shepherd, & M. Davis (Eds), *D. W. Winnicott: Home Is Where We Start From* (pp. 74–90). New York: W. W. Norton, 1986.

Winnicott, D. W. (1969). Berlin Wall. In: C. Winnicott, R. Shepherd, & M. Davis (Eds), *D. W. Winnicott: Home Is Where We Start From* (pp. 221–227). New York: W. W. Norton, 1986.

Wolfenstein, M. (1966). How is mourning possible? *Psychoanalytic Study of the Child, 21*: 93–123.

Wolfenstein, M. (1969). Loss, rage and repetition. *Psychoanalytic Study of the Child, 24*: 432–460.

Yaşın, Ö. (1965). *Oğlum Savaş'a Mektuplar [Letters to My Son Savaş]* (translated for this volume). Nicosia: Çevre Yayınları.

INDEX